Give Me Five! ENGLISH

BASICS

PUPIL'S BOOK

1

S	Hello, friends!	page 4
1	Ready for school!	page 8
2	Happy birthday!	page 18
3	At the circus	page 28
	My project 1: Family	page 38
4	Fantastic food!	page 40
5	Fun on the farm	page 50
6	A day in the park	page 60
	My project 2: Spring	page 70
7	Let's explore my town!	page 72
8	Camping fun!	page 82
9	Day and night	page 92
	My project 3: Holidays	page 102
	Festivals: Bonfire Night	page 104
	Festivals: Valentine's Day	page 105
	Cambridge Exams Practice	page 106

My name is _____.

Donna Shaw • Joanne Ramsden

Course consultants: Rocío Gutiérrez Burgos and Mónica Pérez Is

macmillan
education

Syllabus

		Vocabulary	Grammar	Phonics
S	**Hello, friends!**	Numbers 1–10 Shapes Colours Days of the week	*Hello.* *Goodbye.* *What's your name?* *I'm (Jake).*	
1	**Ready for school!**	Classroom objects More classroom objects	*Where's my (pencil)? It's here.* *Put the (book) on the (shelf).* *in / on / under*	Consonant sound **r**: **r**ed **r**abbit **r**ed **r**uler
2	**Happy birthday!**	Toys Adjectives	*What is it?* *Is it a (bike)? Yes, it is. No, it isn't.* *What's your favourite toy?* *My favourite toy is a (ball).*	Consonant sound **s**: **s**ix **s**nakes **s**low **s**cooter
3	**At the circus**	Parts of the body Describing hair and eyes	*I've got a (red nose).* *I've got (small eyes).* *My friend has got (long hair).* *He's / She's got (blue eyes).*	Consonant sound **h**: **H**elen **h**appy **h**ippo **h**ops
	My project 1: Family	Family members	*Have you got (a brother)?* *Yes, I have. No, I haven't.*	*This is my (father / mother).* *His / Her name is …*
4	**Fantastic food!**	Food Fruit	*I like / don't like (chicken).* *I love (ice cream).* *Do you like (grapes)?* *Yes, I do. No, I don't.*	Consonant sound **j**: **J**im **j**uggles **j**am **j**uice **j**elly
5	**Fun on the farm**	Farm animals Actions	*Can you see a (cow)?* *Yes, I can. No, I can't.* *(Birds) can fly. (Cows) can't climb.*	Consonant sound **sh**: **sh**ush! **sh**out **sh**eep
6	**A day in the park**	Playground objects and nature Prepositions of place	*Where's (Beth)?* *He's / She's (on the swing).* *Where are (Jake and Molly)?* *They're (behind) the (tree).*	Consonant sound **w**: **W**ally **w**orm **w**ashes **w**indows
	My project 2: Spring	Spring animals and plants	*How many (lambs) can you see?* *I can see (seven) lambs.*	*This is my (butterfly). It's (blue).* *My (bird) is near (a bush).*
7	**Let's explore my town!**	Places in the town Transport Numbers 11–20	*There's a (zoo).* *There are (two sweet shops).* *How many (cars) are there?*	Consonant sound **z**: la**z**y **z**ebra **z**oo
8	**Camping fun!**	Clothes Outdoor activities	*What are you wearing?* *I'm wearing (shorts) and a (T-shirt).* *What's he / she doing?* *He's / She's (riding a horse).*	Consonant sound **v**: **V**icky **v**et lo**v**es **v**olleyball
9	**Day and night**	Daily routines Meal times	*I (wash my face) every day.* *I have (dinner in the evening).*	Consonant sound **th**: **th**ree **th**in ba**th** **Th**ursday
	My project 3: Holidays	Places for a holiday Holiday things	*Where do you go on holiday?* *I go to (the beach).*	*I go to the (beach). It's (hot) there.* *I've got (a swimsuit) on my list.*
Festivals		Bonfire Night	Valentine's Day	

| What's this? | What colour is it? | What day is it today? |
| It's a (bike). | It's (green). | It's (Thursday). |

Literacy	Culture	21st Century Skills	Cross-curricular links
A classroom poster	School assemblies	**21st Ways of working:** being organised	**Science:** Tidy classroom; School subjects **Arts and Crafts:** Lines and shapes
A birthday card	Birthday parties in Britain	**21st Ways of thinking:** ordering favourite things	**Science:** The senses **Arts and Crafts:** Patterns
An action rhyme	Circus Day	**21st Ways of working:** working together	**Science:** Parts of the body: bones, joints and muscles **Arts and Crafts:** Lines and colours
Making a class family tree display 👥			**Science:** Different types of family **Arts and Crafts:** Art in my home
A lunch menu	A traditional English breakfast	**21st Living in the world:** eating healthily	**Science:** Healthy food; Meals of the day **Arts and Crafts:** Texture
Animal riddles	Urban farms	**21st Ways of thinking:** putting things in groups	**Science:** Farm animals and domestic animals; How animals move; Wild animals **Arts and Crafts:** Forms
Instructions	Parks in Britain	**21st Living in the world:** being careful in the playground	**Science:** Living and non-living things; What plants need to survive **Arts and Crafts:** Geometric and organic shapes
Making a class spring wall display 👥			**Science:** Living things **Arts and Crafts:** Art in my world
A fable	Cycling in Britain	**21st Digital skills:** reading digital maps	**Science:** Road safety; Rights and rules **Arts and Crafts:** Buildings and symmetry
A postcard	Camping in the garden	**21st Ways of thinking:** thinking before you choose	**Science:** Human and physical elements in the environment; Clothing in different weather **Arts and Crafts:** Landscapes
A poem	The Tooth Fairy	**21st Living in the world:** looking after your teeth	**Science:** Day and night; Parts of the day **Arts and Crafts:** Warm and cool colours
Making a holiday list display 👥			**Science:** Cardinal points; Continents and oceans **Arts and Crafts:** Recycled Art

Cambridge Exams Practice   Practice for the YLE Pre A1 Starters Exam (see p119 for syllabus)

Hello, friends!

1 Listen and point. Sing *What's your name?*

2 Say *The ten balloons* chant. CD1 3

3 Find, count and write.

10	 balloons		  bananas		
	 balls		 hats		  socks
	 books		 dogs		bike

Key learning outcomes: identify and say numbers 1–10
Language: *Hello. Goodbye. What's your name? I'm (Jake).*

1 Listen and repeat. Act out. CD1 4

2 Listen and find. Point. CD1 5

Hello!

Hello!

What's this?

It's a bike. It's for two children.

It's perfect!

3 Point. Ask and answer.

What's this?   It's a balloon.

4 Find these shapes in the picture.

● circle   ▭ rectangle

■ square   ▲ triangle   ⬭ oval

Key learning outcomes: identify and say five shapes
Language: *What's this? It's a (bike).*

1 Listen and read. Act out. CD1 6

A big surprise

Key learning outcomes: read, listen and understand a story about a magic bike
Language: *What colour is it? It's green.*

1 **Listen and sing** *Seven days a week*. CD1 7

Monday, Tuesday,
Wednesday, Thursday,
Friday, Saturday and Sunday.

Seven days a week.
Seven days a week.
We ride our magic bike,
Seven days a week.

2 💬 **Talk Partners** **Listen. Ask and answer.** CD1 8

What day is it today?

It's Thursday.

What day is it today? It's THURSDAY

| MONDAY |
| TUESDAY |
| WEDNESDAY |
| FRIDAY |
| SATURDAY |
| SUNDAY |

Key learning outcomes: ask and answer about days of the week
Language: *What day is it today? It's (Thursday).*

Unit 1 Ready for school!

1 **Listen and point. Sing** *I'm ready for school!* CD1 10

A pen, a pencil,
A crayon, too.
I'm ready! I'm ready!
I'm ready for school!

A rubber, a ruler,
A sharpener, too.
I'm ready! I'm ready!
I'm ready for school!

A book, a school bag,
A pencil case, too.
I'm ready! I'm ready!
I'm ready for school!
Hurray! I'm ready for school!

2 **Read and stick the ten stickers. Listen and say the chant.**  CD1 12

book   pen   rubber   pencil   ruler

📖 **Learning to learn** → Spelling: go to page 15 in your Activity Book.

Key learning outcomes: identify and say ten classroom objects; sing a song about school
Vocabulary: classroom objects

1 Listen and repeat. Act out.

Grammar

Where's my pencil?
It's here.

2 Listen and find. Circle.

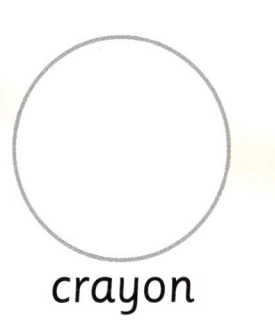
crayon

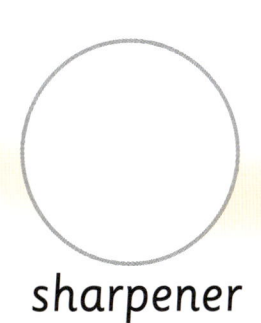
sharpener

computer

school bag

pencil case

Key learning outcomes: use *where's …?* and *here* to locate objects
Grammar: *Where's my (pen)? It's here.*

What classroom objects can you see in the story?

1 Listen and read. Act out. CD1 15

Toby goes to school

1 Look at Toby. He's sad.

Poor Toby. Dogs don't go to school.

2 Look! Toby is on the magic bike.

Stop, Toby!

Oh no! My pencil case!

3 Look! He's in the classroom now.

Be quiet, Toby. The teacher is here.

Key learning outcomes: read, listen and understand a story about Toby in school
Language: *Where's my purple pencil case? Put the pencil case on the desk.*

Now watch the animated story!

After you read

→ Go to page 8 in your Activity Book.

2 **Values** Read and circle.

Keep the classroom tidy.
Put *books* / *crayons* / *rubbish* in the bin.

Values: keeping the classroom tidy

1 Listen, point and say.

 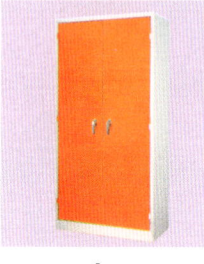    

shelf   cupboard   bin   desk   board   chair

2 Listen and point. Sing *Let's tidy up*.

Put the book on the shelf,
On the shelf, on the shelf.
Put the book on the shelf.
Let's tidy up!

Put the paper in the bin,
In the bin, in the bin.
Put the paper in the bin.
Let's tidy up!

Put the chair under the desk,
Under the desk, under the desk.
Put the chair under the desk.
Let's tidy up!

3 **Talk Partners** Listen and repeat. Play a game.

Put the pencil under the chair.

Good.

Key learning outcomes: give and follow instructions
Vocabulary: classroom objects   **Grammar:** *Put the (paper in the bin).*

1 **Listen and say.** CD1 20

Toby's tongue twister

r – r – r. A **r**ed **r**abbit on a **r**ed **r**uler.

2 **Listen and match.** CD1 21

1

3

2

4

3 **Talk Partners** **Make and play the game.**

Teacher's Resource Bank: Unit 1

Where's the sharpener?

It's in the cupboard.

Key learning outcomes: play a communication game about classroom objects
Phonics: the 'r' sound

Lesson 6 British culture

1 Listen and read. Answer. **CD1 22**

Hello! I'm Alex.

And I'm Lucy. We go to primary school in England. At school, we have an assembly every day.

1 We sit on the floor with all the children in our school. We listen to the head teacher.

2 We play music and we sing songs.

3 We clap our hands when boys and girls do good work.

Think about your culture
What do you do every day at school?

Key learning outcomes: read about school assemblies in Britain; think about what you do at school

 Text type: **A classroom poster**

Before you read

1 Who are the good children? Circle.

2 Listen and read the classroom poster. CD1 24

Class rules

Listen to others.

Put your hand up to speak.

Work quietly.

Sit down on your chair.

Walk in the classroom.

Tidy up your things.

After you read

➡ Go to page **12** in your Activity Book.

Key learning outcomes: read and understand a classroom rules poster

1 Listen and number. Say. CD1 25

book

rubber

ruler

sharpener

computer

pencil

crayon

pen

school bag

pencil case

2 Look, read and circle.

1 The school bag is *in* / *under* the chair.

2 The pencil case is *in* / *on* the school bag.

3 The ruler is *under* / *on* the school bag.

4 The rubber is *under* / *on* the chair.

3 👥 **Cooperative learning** Sing *Well done!* CD1 26

WELL DONE! GIVE ME FIVE!

Key learning outcomes: review language in the unit
Language: classroom objects and prepositions of place

Welcome to Channel 21! This programme is about school. What do you do at school?

1 Watch the video. Number the pictures. ▶

1

2 Watch the video again. Read and tick (✓) or cross (✗). ▶

1 The children read stories. ✓

3 The children run in the classroom.

2 The children sing songs.

4 The children put books in the box.

3 Read and circle.

Being organised

It's important to prepare your school bag.

1 I put my (ruler) / rubber in my school bag.

2 I put my **book** / **pencil case** in my school bag.

3 I put my **book** / **ball** in my school bag.

4 I put my **water** / **snack** in my school bag.

Key learning outcomes: watch and understand a video about school in Britain
21st Ways of working: being organised

seventeen **17**

Unit 2 Happy birthday!

1 Listen and point. Sing *Happy birthday!* CD1 28

Happy birthday!
Happy birthday to you!
Here's a present,
A present for you.

Is it a doll?
Is it a train?
Is it a kite
or a computer game?

Chorus

Is it a robot?
Is it a ball?
Is it a scooter
or a dinosaur?

Chorus

2 Read and stick the ten stickers. Listen and say the chant. CD1 30

ball

train

car

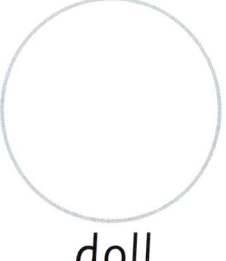
doll

kite

📖 **Learning to learn** ➔ Spelling: go to page 25 in your Activity Book.

Key learning outcomes: identify and say ten toys; sing a song about a birthday present
Vocabulary: toys

1 **Listen and repeat. Act out.** CD1 31

What is it? Is it a bike?

No, it isn't.

Is it a scooter?

Yes, it is!

It's a fantastic present. Thank you!

Happy Birthday

Grammar

What is it?
Is it a bike?
Yes, it is.
No, it isn't.

2 **Listen and circle.** CD1 32

1

2

3

4

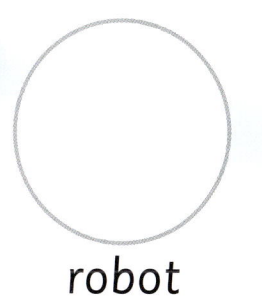

robot

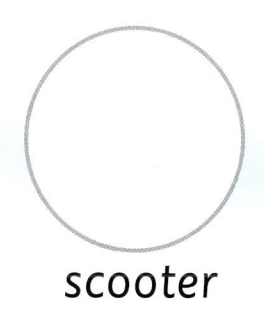

scooter

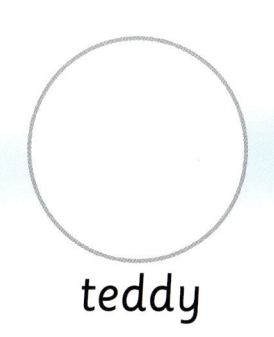

teddy

dinosaur

computer game

Key learning outcomes: use *What is it?*, *Is it a …?*, *Yes, it is. No, it isn't* to identify things.
Grammar: *What is it? Is it a (bike)? Yes, it is. No, it isn't.*

Before you read

How many toys can you see in the story?

1 Listen and read. Act out. CD1 33

The slow scooter

1
Let's have a race.
Good idea!
Ready, steady … go!

2
Oh no! My new scooter is slow. Wait for me!

3
What's the matter, Beth?
My new scooter is slow. The wheels are very small.
I've got an idea.

4
Magic Bike! Magic Bike! Can you help?
Ring Ring

Key learning outcomes: read, listen and understand a story about a new toy
Language: *What is it? It's a motor. My scooter is slow.*

5

6

7

8

Now watch the animated story!

After you read

➡ Go to page 18 in your Activity Book.

2 **Values** Read and circle.

When a person helps you, say *hello / please / thank you*.

1 Listen, point and say.
CD1 34

big   small   old   new   fast   slow

2 Listen and point. Sing *My favourite toy*.
CD1 35

My favourite toy is a train.
My favourite toy is a train.
It's fast. It's new.
It's red and blue.
My favourite toy is a train.

My favourite toy is a teddy.
My favourite toy is a teddy.
It's old. It's big.
It's brown and pink.
My favourite toy is a teddy.

3 💬 **Talk Partners** Listen and repeat. Ask and answer.
CD1 36

What's your favourite toy?

My favourite toy is a ball. It's old.

22 twenty-two

Key learning outcomes: ask and answer questions about favourite toys
Vocabulary: adjectives **Grammar:** *What's your favourite toy? My favourite toy is a (ball).*

1 Listen and say. CD1 38

Toby's tongue twister

s – s – s. **S**ix **s**nakes on a **s**low **s**cooter.

2 Listen and number. CD1 39

1

3 👥 **Cooperative learning** Sing *Sharing is a good thing to do*. CD1 40

4 💬 **Talk Partners** Make and play the game.

Teacher's Resource Bank: Unit 2

My favourite toy is new.

Is it a bike?

No, it isn't.

Is it a scooter?

Yes, it is.

Key learning outcomes: play a communication game about toys
Phonics: the 's' sound

Lesson 6 British culture

1 Listen and read. Answer.

CD1 41

> It's my birthday today. I'm seven. I have a party on my birthday.

1

My party is a fancy dress party. Look! We're pirates today.

2

I've got lots of birthday cards. They're fantastic!

3

I play party games in the garden with my friends. It's good fun!

4

I've got a birthday cake with seven candles.

Think about your culture

Do you have a party on your birthday?

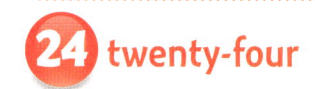

Key learning outcomes: read about birthday parties in Britain; think about your birthday party

 Text type: **A birthday card**

Before you read

1 What can you see on the birthday card? Circle and say.

dog   seven   (bike)   dinosaur   scooter

kite

present   balloons   six   birthday cake

2 Listen and read the birthday card. CD1 43

To Beth,

Happy Birthday

Have a fantastic party with your friends.

Lots of love, from Mum and Dad x x x

After you read

→ Go to page **22** in your Activity Book.

1 Listen and number. Say. CD1 44

car

teddy

scooter

kite

doll

ball

robot

train

dinosaur

computer game

2 Look, read and circle.

1 My favourite toy is old and brown. *teddy* / *train*

2 My favourite toy is new and green. *doll* / *dinosaur*

3 My favourite toy is big and purple. *robot* / *scooter*

4 My favourite toy is fast and blue. *car* / *kite*

3 👥 Cooperative learning Sing *Well done!*  CD1 45

WELL DONE! GIVE ME FIVE!

Key learning outcomes: review language in the unit
Language: toys and adjectives

> Hello again. Today's programme is about toys. What's your favourite toy?

1 Watch the video. Tick (✓) or cross (✗). Are these toys in the video? ▶

2 Watch the video again. Read and circle. ▶

1 The teddy is *grey* / *red*.

2 The dinosaurs are *big* / *small*.

3 The green scooter is *fast* / *slow*.

4 Abby's favourite toy is a *kite* / *ball*.

3 Read and think. Write *1*, *2* and *3*.

Ordering

1 = 😄   2 = 🙂   3 = 🙂

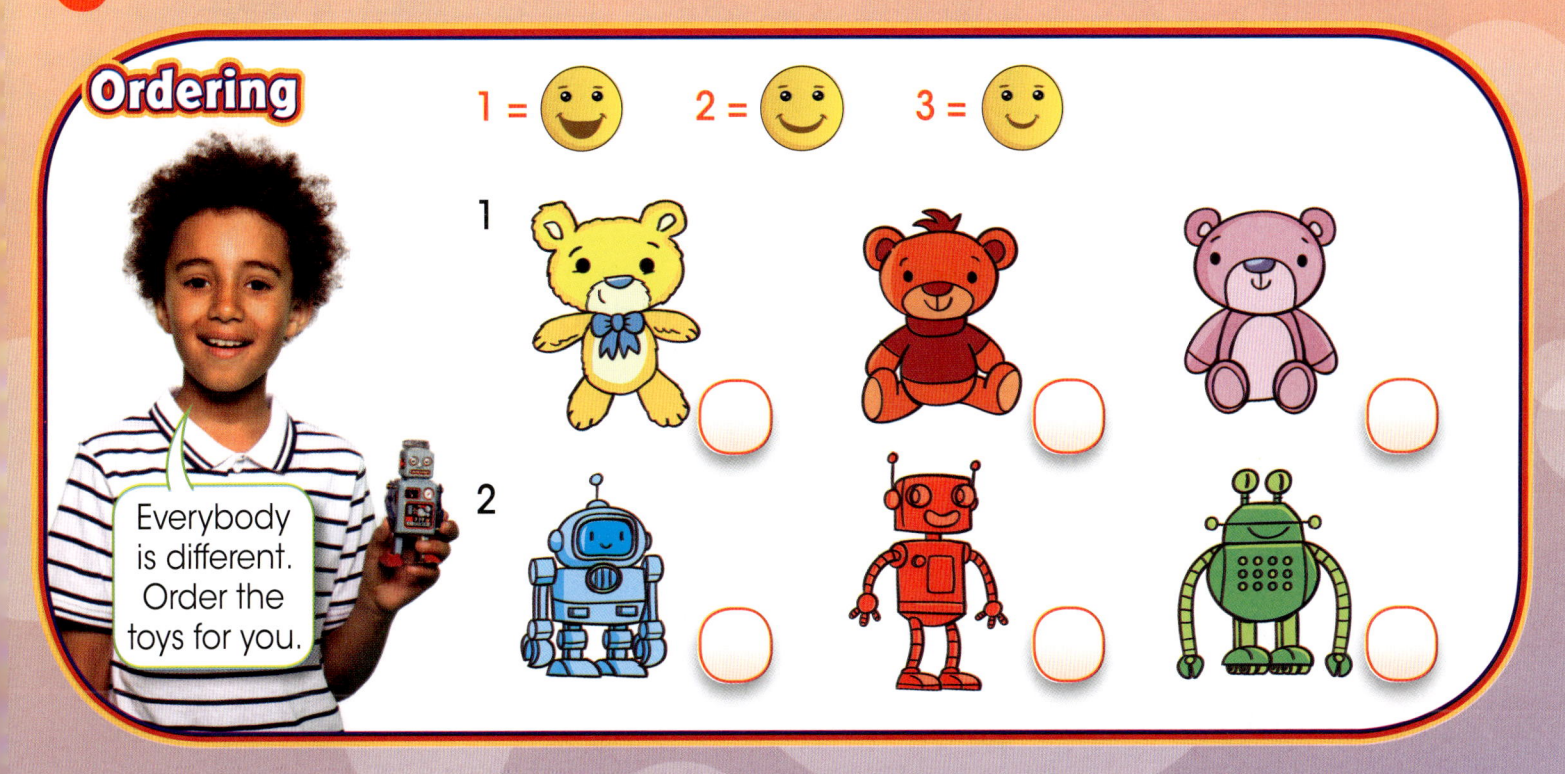

> Everybody is different. Order the toys for you.

Key learning outcomes: watch and understand a video about favourite toys
21st Ways of thinking: ordering favourite things

twenty-seven **27**

1 Listen and point. Sing *This is me*.  CD1 47

This is my body,
This is me.
This is my body.
Count with me.

Two feet,
Ten toes,
Two eyes,
One big nose.

Chorus

Ten fingers,
One head,
Two arms,
Two long legs.

WELCOME TO THE CIRCUS

2 Read and stick the ten stickers. Listen and say the chant. CD1 49

head

legs

feet

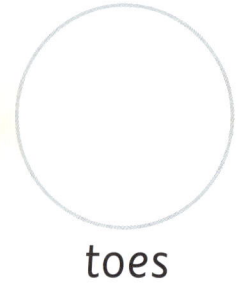
toes

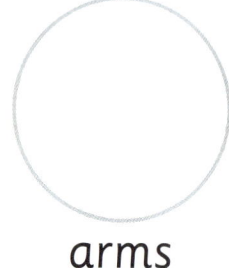
arms

📖 **Learning to learn** ➡ Spelling: go to page 35 in your Activity Book.

Key learning outcomes: identify and say ten parts of the body; sing a song about the body
Vocabulary: parts of the body

1 **Listen and repeat. Act out.** CD1 50

Look at me! I've got a red nose.

I've got big ears.

And I've got a big mouth. I'm a clown.

I'm a clown, too.

Grammar

I've got a red nose.
I've got big ears.

2 **Listen and draw.** CD1 51

1  2  3  4

 ears

 mouth

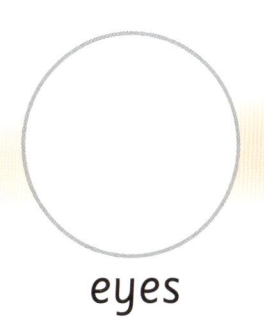 eyes

 nose

 fingers

Key learning outcomes: use *I've got …* for parts of the body
Grammar: *I've got (a big nose). I've got (small eyes).*

Before you read

Can you see a clown in the story?

1 Listen and read. Act out.

Fun at the circus

1

I can't juggle.

Let's make a circus. Magic Bike, can you help?

2

Welcome to the circus, children.

Wow! This circus is very big.

3

Here's Annie the acrobat.

She's fantastic!

4

And here's Molly the clown.

Wow!

Look at me! I've got big feet and I've got purple hair.

Key learning outcomes: read, listen and understand a story about a circus
Language: *I've got big feet. He's got purple hair.*

5 And now here's amazing Toby!

Wow! He's very strong.

6 And now here's Jake and his magic bike!

Look! I've got one hand on the bike.

Be careful, Jake!

7 I'm not an acrobat. Help!

Oh no!

CRASH!

8 Are you OK, Jake?

Yes, I am. Look! We're in the garden again.

But look at Toby! He's got purple hair!

Now watch the animated story!

After you read

➔ **Go to page 28 in your Activity Book.**

2 **Values** Read and circle.

When you ride a bike, wear a helmet and use two *hands* / *fingers* / *toes*.

Values: riding a bike safely

1 Listen, point and say. CD2 1

    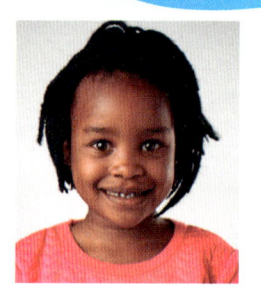 

long hair　　short hair　　blonde hair　　brown hair　　black hair　　red hair

2 Listen and point. Sing *My friend*.  CD2 2

I've got a friend called Jake.
He's got green eyes.
He's got short hair.
He's fantastic!

*We're different
And that's OK.
We're different.
And we're friends.*

I've got a friend called Beth.
She's got brown eyes.
She's got long hair.
She's fantastic!

3 💬 **Talk Partners** Listen and repeat. Talk about your friend. CD2 3

My friend has got black hair.

My friend has got green eyes.

Key learning outcomes: describe a friend's hair and eyes
Vocabulary: adjectives to describe hair **Grammar:** *My friend has got (long hair). She's got (blue eyes).*

1 Listen and say.

CD2 5

h – h – h. **H**elen the **h**appy **h**ippo **h**ops and **h**ops.

2 Listen and number.

CD2 6

1

3 Talk Partners Make and play the game.

Teacher's Resource Bank: Unit 3

My clown has got short hair.

And he's got big eyes.

Key learning outcomes: play a communication game describing people
Phonics: the 'h' sound

1 Listen and read. Answer.  CD2 7

'Circus Day' is a special day at our school. We paint our faces. We do different circus activities, too.

1 I spin a plate. It's very difficult. Look!

2 I juggle scarves. Oh no! It's fun!

3 I ride a special bike. My teacher helps me.

4 I walk on stilts. Look! I've got long legs.

💡 **Think about your culture**

Do you go to the circus with your family?

Key learning outcomes: read about Circus Day in British schools; think about a circus where you live

 Text type: **An action rhyme**

Before you read

1 How are you today? Circle.

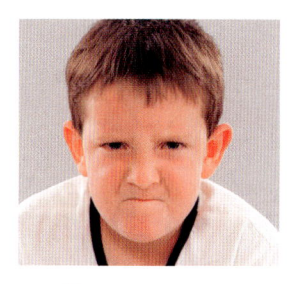

I'm happy.   I'm sad.   I'm angry.   I'm tired.

2 Listen and read the rhyme. CD2 9

My feelings

When I'm sad,
I sit and cry.

When I'm happy,
I laugh and smile.

When I'm angry,
I stamp my feet.

When I'm tired,
I go to sleep.

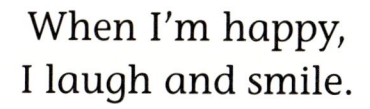

3 👥 **Cooperative learning** Sing *We can do it!*  CD2 10

After you read

➜ Go to page **32** in your Activity Book.

1 Listen and number. Say. CD2 11

mouth

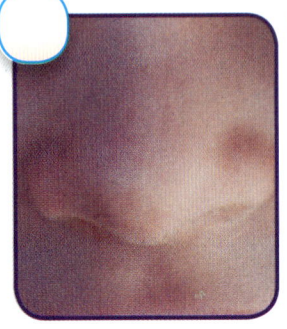
nose

arms

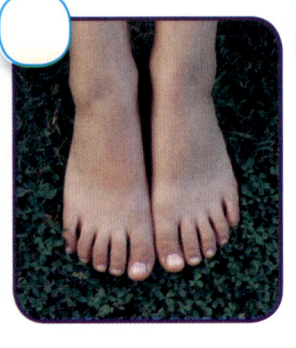
feet

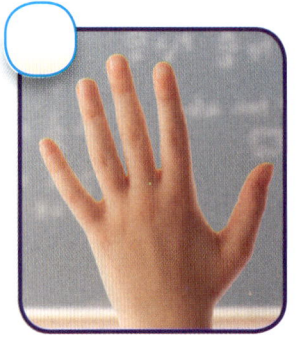
fingers

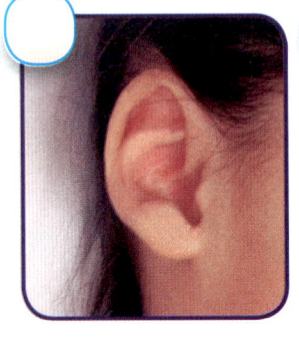
ears

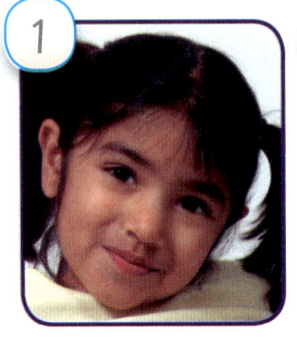
head

legs

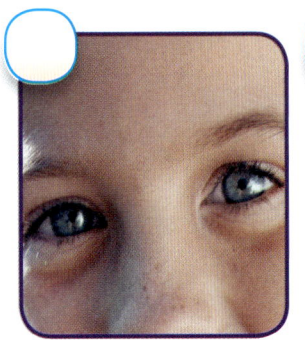
eyes

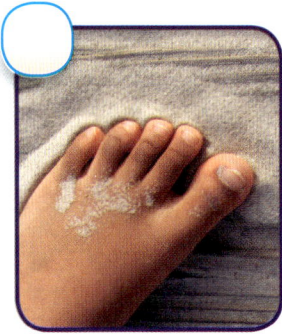
toes

2 Read and circle **A** or **B**.

1 She's got long hair. （A）/ **B**

2 He's got short hair. **A** / **B**

3 He's got brown eyes. **A** / **B**

4 She's got green eyes. **A** / **B**

3 👥 **Cooperative learning** Sing *Well done!* CD2 12

WELL DONE! GIVE ME FIVE!

Key learning outcomes: review language in the unit
Language: parts of the body and *He's / She's got …*

Hello again. Today's programme is about the circus. Do you like the circus?

1 Watch the video. Number the pictures. ▶

1

2 Watch the video again. Read and tick (✓) or cross (✗). ▶

1 The circus is blue and yellow.  ✓

3 The man rides a special bike.

2 The man spins four plates.

4 The boy and girl work together.

3 Read and circle.

Working together

It's fun to work and play together with your friends.

1 We play *video games* / *football* together.

2 We *write* / *draw pictures* together.

3 We *play music* / *sing songs* together.

4 We *clean the car* / *tidy up* together.

Key learning outcomes: watch and understand a video about the circus
21st Ways of working: working together

FAMILY
Make a class family tree display

Learn

1 Listen and point. Say. CD2 14

1 grandmother
2 grandfather
3 father
4 mother
5 uncle
6 aunt
7 brother
8 sister
9 cousins

2 💬 **Talk Partners** Listen. Ask and answer. Write the numbers. CD2 15

Have you got a brother?

Yes, I have. I've got two brothers.

Have you got a sister?

No, I haven't.

	brothers	sisters	aunts	uncles	cousins
my friend					

Plan your project

Prepare to make a family leaf.
Go to page 36 in your Activity Book.

Digital tip!

Look for pictures of leaves on the Internet. What colours can you see?

Key learning outcomes: identify and talk about family members
Language: *Have you got a (brother)? Yes, I have.*

Create

1 Read. Make a family leaf.

1

2

Cut out your leaf.
Colour your leaf.

Stick your family photo on
the leaf. Write on the leaf.

Show and tell

2 **Cooperative learning** Sing *It's fun to work together.*  CD2 16

3 Make a family tree with the class. Listen. Tell the class about
your family.  CD2 17

This is my happy family. This is my
mother. Her name is Marta. This is
my brother. His name is Ben.

How old is Ben?

He's four.

OUR FAMILY TREE

Think about your project

 Go to page 37 in your Activity Book.

Key learning outcomes: make a family leaf; present a class tree display
Language: *This is my (mother). Her name is (Marta).*

1 Listen and point. Sing *Delicious food*.  CD2 18

I've got rice and eggs
And chicken today.
Delicious food
At the Astro Café!

I've got fish and chips
And salad today.
Delicious food
At the Astro Café!

I've got fruit and cake
And ice cream today.
Delicious food
At the Astro Café!

2 Read and stick the ten stickers. Listen and say the chant.  CD2 20

eggs

meat

fish

chips

rice

📖 **Learning to learn** ➡ Spelling: go to page 47 in your Activity Book.

Key learning outcomes: identify and say food; sing a song about food
Vocabulary: food

1 Listen and repeat. Act out.  CD2 21

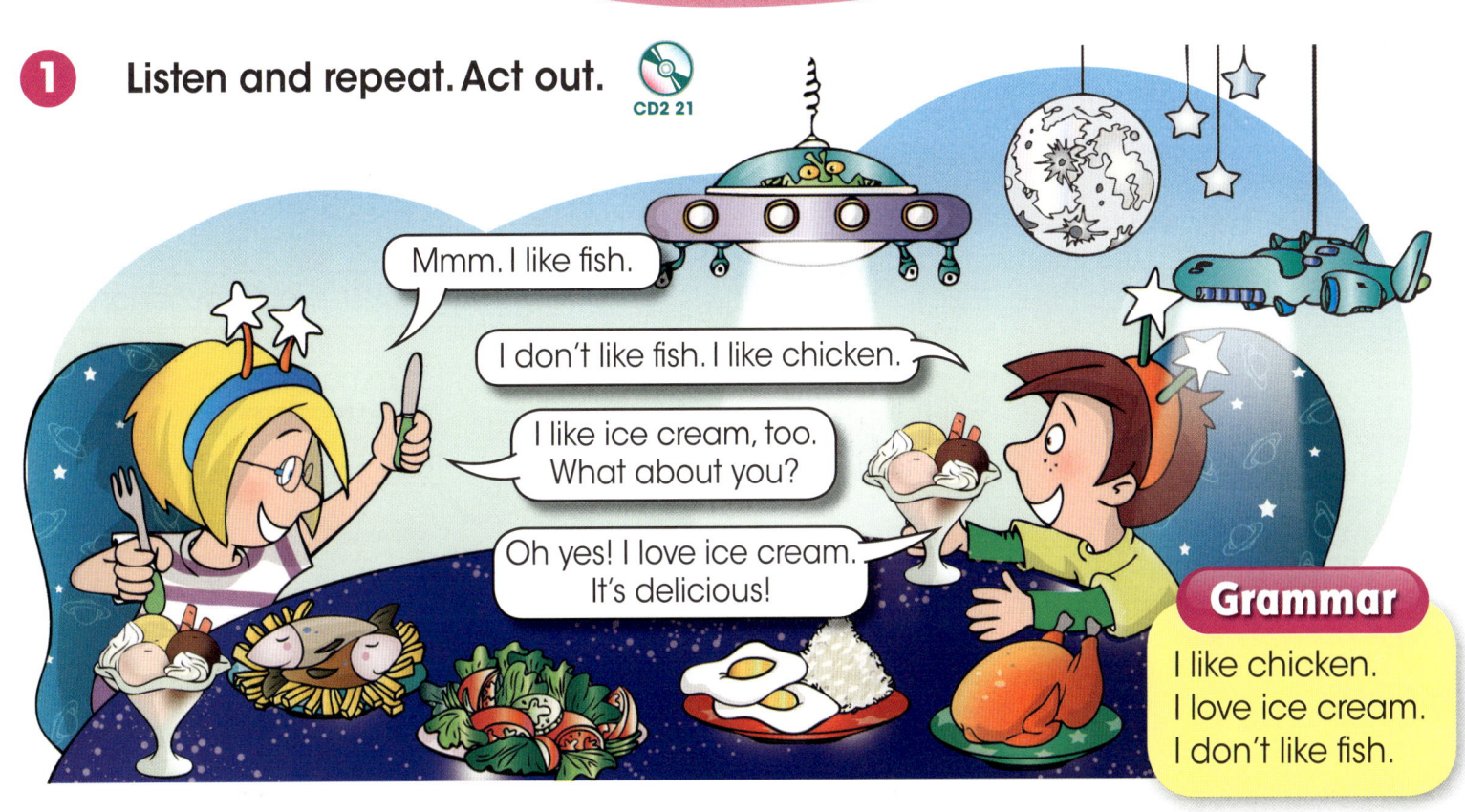

Mmm. I like fish.

I don't like fish. I like chicken.

I like ice cream, too. What about you?

Oh yes! I love ice cream. It's delicious!

Grammar

I like chicken.
I love ice cream.
I don't like fish.

2 Listen and draw a mouth. CD2 22

love 😊 like 🙂 don't like 🙁

1
2
3

4
5
6

fruit   cake   salad   chicken   ice cream

Key learning outcomes: use *like*, *don't like* and *love* to describe preferences
Grammar: *I like (fruit). I love (ice cream). I don't like (cake).*

forty-one **41**

Before you read

What food can you see in the story?

1 Listen and read. Act out. CD2 23

I'm hungry

1

Let's play! Hello, Molly and Jake. Welcome to my restaurant.

Hello! A table for two, please.

2

This food isn't real. I'm hungry.

I'm hungry, too.

I know. Let's ring the bell.

3

Wow! The food is real now.

And look! The waiter is a robot.

I love robots.

4

Here you are, Molly. Here you are, Beth.

Thank you. I like ice cream.

And I love chocolate cake. It's my favourite.

Key learning outcomes: read, listen and understand a story about a magic restaurant
Language: *I love cake. I don't like oranges. Do you like peaches? No, I don't.*

5 And here's an orange for you, Jake.

But I don't like oranges.

6 Do you like peaches?

No, I don't.

Do you like grapes?

No, I don't. I don't like fruit!

7 No problem. One minute …

Wow! Robot, you're amazing!

8 Here's a delicious fruit juice for you, Jake.

Mmm. I love fruit juice! Thank you, robot.

Now watch the animated story!

After you read

➔ Go to page 40 in your Activity Book.

2 **Values** Read and circle.

It's important to eat *ice cream* / *meat* / *fruit* every day.

1 Listen, point and say. CD2 24

mango ⌐ grape   peach   cherry   lemon   coconut

2 Listen and point. Sing *Do you like fruit?* CD2 25

I like grapes.
What about you?
Do you like grapes?
Do you like fruit?

I like grapes.
Yes, I do.
Eating fruit is fun to do.

I like peaches.
What about you?
Do you like peaches?
Do you like fruit?

I like peaches.
Yes, I do.
Eating fruit is fun to do.

3 💬 **Talk Partners** Listen and repeat. Ask and answer. CD2 26

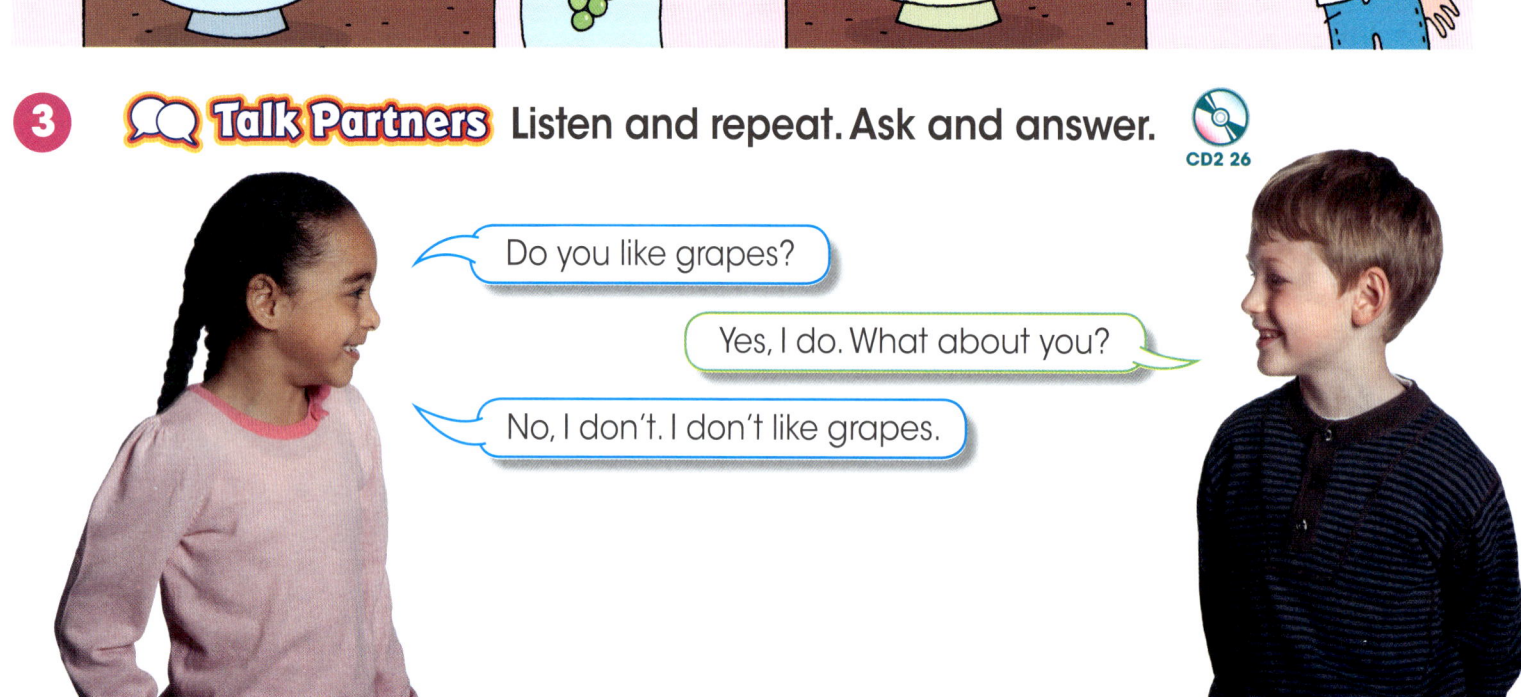

Do you like grapes?

Yes, I do. What about you?

No, I don't. I don't like grapes.

Key learning outcomes: ask and answer questions to find out what fruit people like
Vocabulary: fruit **Grammar:** *Do you like (grapes)? Yes, I do. No, I don't.*

1 **Listen and say.** CD2 28

Toby's tongue twister

j – j – j. **J**im **j**uggles **j**am, **j**uice and **j**elly.

2 **Listen and match.** CD2 29

1

2

3

3 💬 **Talk Partners** Make and play the game.

Teacher's Resource Bank: Unit 4

Do you like chicken?

Yes, I do.

Do you like ice cream?

Yes, I do.

Do you like chicken ice cream?

No, I don't.

4 👥 **Cooperative learning** Sing *Calm down.*  CD2 30

Key learning outcomes: play a communication game about food
Phonics: the 'j' sound

1 Listen and read. Answer.

CD2 31

It's Sunday morning. Let's make a traditional English breakfast today.

1

Here are the ingredients: eggs, mushrooms, baked beans, tomatoes and bread.

2

I mix the eggs. Lucy makes the toast. Dad cuts the tomatoes.

3

Dad cooks the food. We prepare the tray.

4

We take the breakfast to Mum. She's in bed. She's very happy.

Think about your culture

What do you have for breakfast?

Key learning outcomes: read about a traditional English breakfast; think about what you have for breakfast

 Text type: **A lunch menu**

Before you read

1 Read, look and circle. How many days is the menu for?

a one day   b three days   c five days

2 Listen and read the lunch menu. CD2 33

Munch! Munch! Munch!
I like a healthy lunch!

Lunch Menu

Monday	Tuesday	Wednesday	Thursday	Friday
salad	carrots	soup	salad	soup
meat and vegetables	chicken and pasta	meat and rice	chicken and potatoes	fish and salad
jelly	fruit	ice cream	fruit salad	carrot cake

After you read

→ Go to page 44 in your Activity Book.

Key learning outcomes: read and understand a lunch menu

1 Listen and number. Say. CD2 34

meat

fruit

eggs

salad

chicken

chips

fish

cake

rice

ice cream

2 Read and circle for you.

1 I *like* / *don't like* / *love* salad.

2 I *like* / *don't like* / *love* eggs.

3 I *like* / *don't like* / *love* cake.

4 I *like* / *don't like* / *love* fish.

5 I *like* / *don't like* / *love* fruit.

I love salad.

3 🗣 **Cooperative learning** Sing *Well done!* CD2 35

WELL DONE! GIVE ME FIVE!

Key learning outcomes: review language in the unit
Language: food, *love, like* and *don't like*

21 CHANNEL

Today's programme is about school lunches. Do you have a healthy lunch?

1 Watch the video. Tick (✓) or cross (✗). Are these lunches in the video?

✓

2 Watch the video again. Read and circle. ▶

1 The children (like) / **don't like** the lunch.

3 The teddy has got **big** / **small** eyes.

2 There is a **bird** / **cat** lunch.

4 Abby's lunch **is** / **isn't** healthy.

3 Read and think. Tick (✓) or cross (✗).

Healthy eating

It's important to eat healthy food every day.

1 It's important to eat fruit and vegetables. ✓

2 It's important to eat cake.

3 It's important to eat rice and pasta.

4 It's important to drink water.

Key learning outcomes: watch and understand a video about school lunches
21st Living in the world: eating healthily

forty-nine **49**

Unit 5 Fun on the farm

1 **Listen and point. Sing *On the farm.*** CD2 37

Animals, animals.
We love animals.
Animals, animals,
On the farm.

Can you see a duck?
Can you see a cat?
Yes, I can! Yes, I can!
The duck is yellow
And the cat is black.

Can you see a horse?
Can you see a cow?
Yes, I can! Yes, I can!
The horse is grey
And the cow is brown.

Can you see a sheep?
Can you see a mouse?
Yes, I can! Yes, I can!
The sheep is white
And the mouse is brown.

2 **Read and stick the ten stickers. Listen and say the chant.** CD2 39

cat

( )

cow

( )

bird

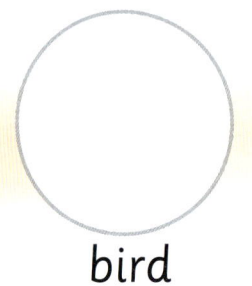

frog

goat

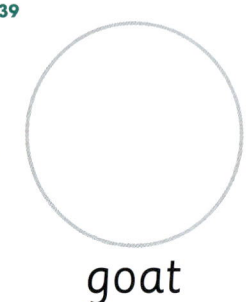

📖 **Learning to learn** ➡ Spelling: go to page 57 in your Activity Book.

Key learning outcomes: identify and say ten farm animals; sing a song about the farm
Vocabulary: farm animals

1 Listen and repeat. Act out. CD2 40

Grammar

Can you see Toby?
Yes, I can.
No, I can't.

2 Listen and colour the animals they can see. CD2 41

horse   sheep   duck   mouse   chicken

Key learning outcomes: use *Can you …?* and *Yes, I can. No, I can't.*
Grammar: *Can you see (a cow)? Yes, I can. No, I can't.*

Before you read

What animals can you see in the story?

1 **Listen and read. Act out.** CD2 42

Animal magic

1

Look. Here's Toby.

Oh no! He can see the cat!

2

The cat is on the magic bike. Shoo!

Ring Ring

Stop, Toby!

3 Suddenly ...

Look. Is it a cow?

Yes, it is. But cows can't fly.

It's magic!

4

And look! Is it a goat?

Yes, it is. But goats can't swim.

Amazing!

Key learning outcomes: read, listen and understand a story about a magic farm
Language: *Cows can't fly. This sheep can climb trees. Can you see a cat? Yes, I can.*

Now watch the animated story!

After you read

→ Go to page 50 in your Activity Book.

2 **Values** Read and circle.

Remember! Wash your *face / hands / feet* after you touch animals.

1 Listen, point and say.  CD2 43

fly swim run walk climb jump

2 Listen and point. Sing *Cats can't fly*.  CD2 44

I love cats.
Cats can fly.
No! No! No!
Cats can't fly.
Cats can climb.

I love frogs.
Frogs can run.
No! No! No!
Frogs can't run.
Frogs can jump.

I love cows.
Cows can talk.
No! No! No!
Cows can't talk.
Cows can walk.

3 💬 **Talk Partners** Listen and repeat. Play a game. CD2 45

Cats can fly.

No!

Cats can swim.

Yes!

Key learning outcomes: say what animals can and can't do
Vocabulary: actions **Grammar:** *(Birds) can fly. (Cows) can't climb.*

1 Listen and say. CD2 47

Toby's tongue twister

sh – sh – sh. Shush! Don't **sh**out, **sh**eep!

2 Listen. Tick or cross.   can ✓   can't ✗   CD2 48

1	2	3	4
swim	fly	run	jump
✓	◯	◯	◯

3 👥 **Cooperative learning** Sing *Let's take turns.*  CD2 49

4 💬 **Talk Partners** Make and play the game.

Teacher's Resource Bank: Unit 5

Cats can swim.

Correct. It's my turn now.

Can you make 10 sentences?

Key learning outcomes: play a communication game about what animals can do
Phonics: the 'sh' sound

1 Listen and read. Answer. CD2 50

There's a farm in our town. Schools and families can visit the farm. It's very interesting.

1 I love the goats on the farm. I can feed them. Look. This goat is very hungry.

2 I love the horses. This horse is small and it's got lots of hair. Its name is Bob.

3 We can see chickens on the farm. I help the farmer to collect the eggs.

4 I like the garden. Fruit and vegetables grow here. Look. Here are some delicious carrots.

Think about your culture
Can you visit a farm in your country?

Key learning outcomes: read about urban farms in Britain; think about farms where you live

Text type: **Animal riddles**

Before you read

1 Think and draw. Tell your partner.

Three farm animals with two legs

Three farm animals with four legs

2 Listen and read. Answer the riddles.
CD2 52

Mrsgreenenglishclassblog

Fun zone   Homework zone   Class zone

MRS GREEN

Read the riddles. Can you guess the animals?

I've got two legs.
I can swim.
I can fly.
I'm small and brown.
What am I?

I've got four legs.
I can walk.
I can't climb.
I'm big.
I'm black and white.
What am I?

After you read

→ Go to page **54** in your Activity Book.

1 Listen and number. Say. CD2 53

1 				
chicken	mouse	sheep	frog	bird

cat	horse	duck	cow	goat

2 Look at the pictures. Circle the animal.

1 This animal can jump. It's green.　　*frog* / *goat*

2 This animal can fly. It's black.　　*mouse* / *bird*

3 This animal can't fly. It's white.　　*duck* / *sheep*

4 This animal can swim. It's white.　　*cow* / *duck*

5 This animal can't climb. It's orange.　*cat* / *chicken*

6 This animal can run. It's black.　　*horse* / *goat*

3 👥 **Cooperative learning** Sing *Well done!*  CD2 54

Key learning outcomes: review language in the unit
Language: farm animals, *can* and *can't*

Hello again. Today's programme is about farm animals. What's your favourite farm animal?

1 **Watch the video. Number the pictures.** ▶

○ ○ ○ 1

2 **Watch the video again. Read and tick (✓) or cross (✗).** ▶

1 The cow has got small ears. ✗

2 The sheep has got a long nose. ○

3 The lamb is tired. ○

4 Chickens can fly. ○

3 **Read and tick (✓).**

Grouping

Putting things into groups helps you to think.

1

They can climb. ○

They can jump. ○

They can fly. ○

2

They have got hair. ○

They have got two legs. ○

They have got a tail. ○

Key learning outcomes: watch and understand a video about farm animals
21st Ways of thinking: putting things in groups

fifty-nine **59**

Unit 6 A day in the park

1 **Listen and point. Sing** *It's fun in the park.*  CD3 1

We can climb a tree.
We can jump and run.
We can play on the swing.
The park is fun.

It's fun, fun, fun in the park.
Yes, it's fun, fun, fun in the park.

We can play on the slide.
We can jump and run.
We can play on the roundabout.
The park is fun.

Chorus

We can play on the grass.
We can jump and run.
We can play on the seesaw.
The park is fun.

Chorus

2 **Read and stick the ten stickers. Listen and say the chant.** CD3 3

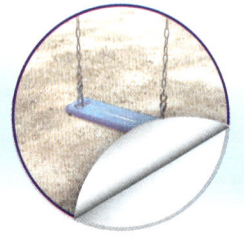 swing

slide

seesaw

roundabout

climbing frame

📖 **Learning to learn** ➡ **Spelling: go to page 67 in your Activity Book.**

Key learning outcomes: identify and say ten park objects; sing a song about playing in the park
Vocabulary: park objects

1 Listen and repeat. Act out. CD3 4

Grammar

Where's my sister?
She's on the swing.

Where's my brother?
He's on the roundabout.

2 Listen and match. CD3 5

grass   flower   tree   bush   rock

Key learning outcomes: use *where* and prepositions of place
Grammar: *Where's (Beth)? She's (on the swing). Where's (Jake)? He's (on the slide).*

Before you read

What can you see in the playground?

1   **Listen and read. Act out.**   CD3 6

Hide and seek

Key learning outcomes: read, listen and understand a story about a game of hide and seek
Language: *Where's Toby? He's on the slide. Where are Jake and Molly? They're behind the tree.*

5 Later …

Oh no! Where's Toby?

I don't know. Toby! Toby!

I can't see him in the park.

6

He isn't under the bush.

And he isn't in the long grass.

Magic Bike, can you help?

Ring Ring

7

Now I can see Toby.

Where is he?

He's on the slide!

8

You can't go in the playground, Toby.

But you can have a ride on the magic bike. Let's go!

▶ Now watch the animated story!

After you read

➜ Go to page **60** in your Activity Book.

2 **Values** Read and circle.

Remember! *Respect / Write / Say* the signs around you.

NO DOGS IN THIS AREA

Values: respecting signs

1 **Listen, point and say.** CD3 7

| behind the tree | near the grass | in front of the flowers | next to the bush | between the rocks |

2 **Listen and point. Sing *Hide and seek*.**  CD3 8

Hide, hide,
Hide everyone.
Ready or not,
Here I come!

Where are Jake and Molly?
Where are they?
They're next to the tree.
Let's play again!

Where are Beth and Molly?
Where are they?
They're near the rocks.
Let's play again!

Where are Jake and Beth?
Where are they?
They're behind the bush.
Let's play again!

3 🗨 **Talk Partners** **Listen and repeat. Ask and answer.** CD3 9

Where are Anna and David?

They're in front of the desk.

Key learning outcomes: ask and answer questions to find out where people are
Vocabulary: prepositions of place **Grammar:** *Where are (Jake and Molly)? They're (next to the tree).*

1 Listen and say. CD3 11

Toby's tongue twister

w – w – w. **W**ally the **w**orm **w**ashes **w**indows.

2 Listen and match. CD3 12

1

2

3

4

3 🤝 **Cooperative learning** Sing *Listen to others*. CD3 13

Teacher's Resource Bank: Unit 6

4 💬 **Talk Partners** Make and play the game.

Where are Molly and Toby?

They're between the bushes.

Key learning outcomes: play a communication game about finding people
Phonics: the 'w' sound

Lesson 6 British culture

1 **Listen and read. Answer.** CD3 14

> I love the park in my town. It's very big.
> I go with my family on Saturday.
> We do lots of fun activities.

1 We play cricket on the grass.
Look. I can hit the ball.

2 We feed the ducks on the
pond. They love bread.

3 We ride on the train.
It's great!

4 We love the playground.
The zip wire is very fast.

💡 **Think about your culture**
What do you do at the park?

Key learning outcomes: read about parks in Britain;
think about parks where you live

Text type: **Instructions**

Before you read

1 What do you need to grow flowers? Think and circle.

soil

grass

a book

seeds

water

sun

2 Listen and read the instructions.
CD3 16

My garden

Pansy

They're easy and fun to grow!

Ask an adult to help you. Do not eat seeds.

Instructions

1 Put the soil in a pot.

2 Push the seeds into the soil with your finger.

3 Water the seeds.

4 Put the pot in a sunny place. Watch the plants grow.

5 Put the plants in the garden. Watch the flowers grow.

After you read

→ Go to page 64 in your Activity Book.

1 Listen and number. Say. CD3 17

grass

1

swing

slide

flower

roundabout

seesaw

rock

bush

tree

climbing frame

2 Look, read and circle.

in front of   next to   behind

1 Where's Toby? He's **behind** / **in front of** a rock.

2 Where's Molly? She's **next to** / **in front of** a bush.

3 Where are Beth and Jake? They're **in front of** / **next to** a rock.

3 🧑‍🤝‍🧑 Cooperative learning Sing *Well done!* CD3 18

WELL DONE! GIVE ME FIVE!

Key learning outcomes: review language in the unit
Language: park objects, *Where's / Where are* and prepositions

Today's programme is about playgrounds. Do you like playgrounds? What do you do there?

1 Watch the video. Tick (✓) or cross (✗). Are these playgrounds in the video? ▶

2 Watch the video again. Read and circle. ▶

1 The orange roundabout is *fast* / *slow*.

2 The girl goes *up* / *down* the slide.

3 A *boy* / *girl* is on the zip wire.

4 The climbing frame *is* / *isn't* high.

3 Read and circle.

Being careful

Be careful in the playground.

1 Only go *up* / *down* the slide.

2 Use *two hands* / *one hand* on the swing.

3 *Stand up* / *Sit down* on the seesaw.

4 Wait *in front of* / *next to* the zip wire.

Key learning outcomes: watch and understand a video about playgrounds
21st Living in the world: being careful in the playground

sixty-nine 69

SPRING
Make a spring wall display

Learn

1 Listen and say. Read, count and write. **CD3 20**

 **3** lambs   ⬜ flowers    ⬜ birds

 ⬜ rabbits   ⬜ chicks   ⬜ butterflies

2 💬 **Talk Partners** Listen. Ask and answer. **CD3 21**

How many lambs can you see?

I can see three lambs.

Plan your project

 Prepare to make a spring wall display. Go to page 68 in your Activity Book.

Digital tip!
Look for pictures of spring on the Internet. What can you see?

Key learning outcomes: identify and talk about spring animals and plants
Language: *How many (lambs) can you see? I can see (three) lambs.*

Create

1   **Cooperative learning** Sing *What do I need to do?*  CD3 22

2   **Read. Make a spring animal.**

Cut out your spring animal. Be careful with the scissors!

Colour your spring animal. Use different colours.

Show and tell

3   **Create your wall display. Listen. Tell the class about your animal and stick it on the wall display.**  CD3 23

This is my butterfly. It's brown, pink, orange and blue.

My bird is near a bush.

Think about your project

 Go to page 69 in your Activity Book.

Key learning outcomes: make a spring animal; present a class spring display
Language: *This is my (butterfly). It's (blue). My (bird) is near (a bush).*

Let's explore my town!

1 Listen and point. Sing *Let's go to town.*  CD3 24

Stand up.
Sit down.
Let's go to town
To see what we can see.

There's a cinema.
There's a bookshop, too.
There's a hospital
And there's a swimming pool.

Chorus

There's a supermarket.
There's a sweet shop, too.
There's a restaurant.
And look! There's a zoo!

Chorus

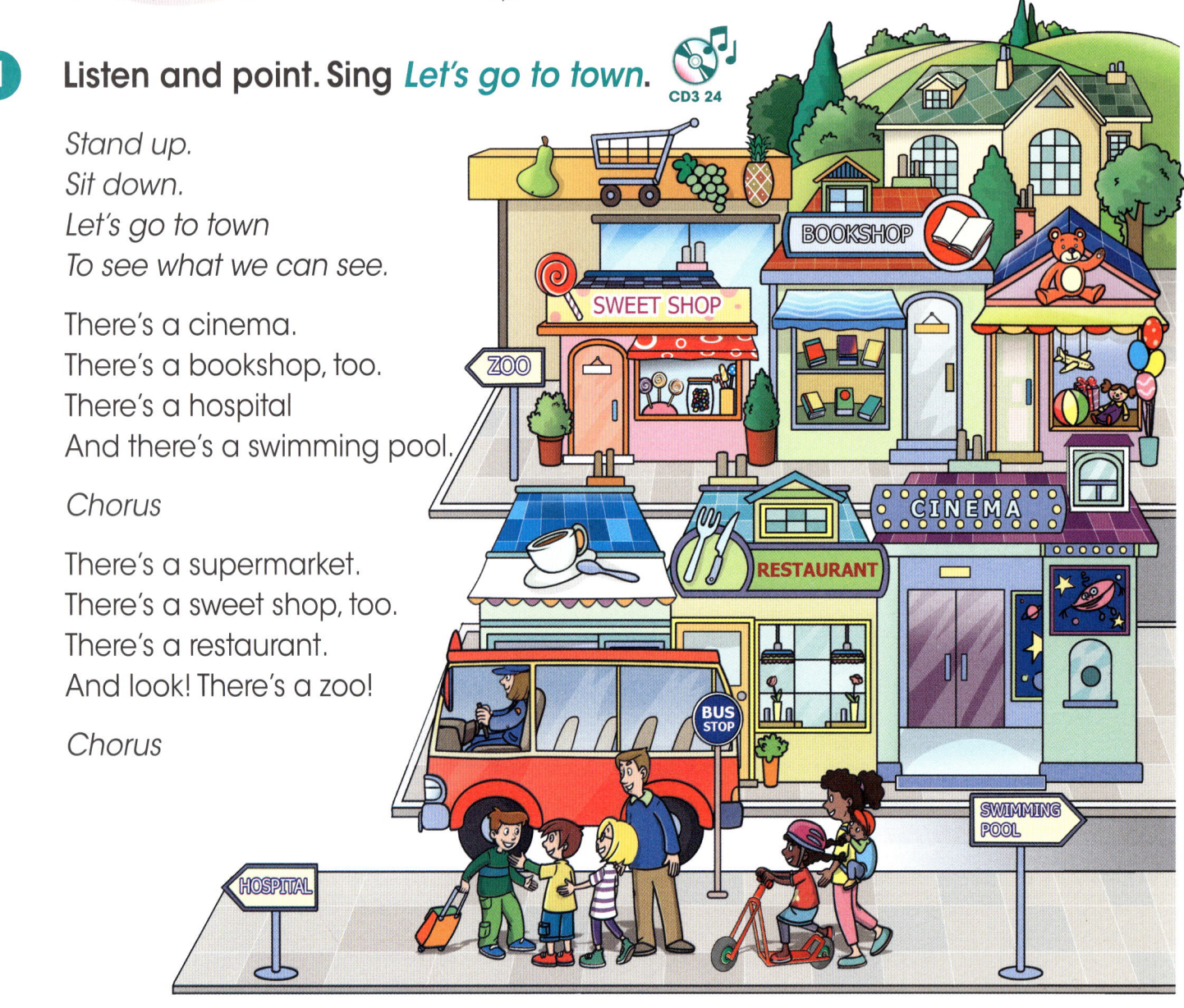

2 Read and stick the ten stickers. Listen and say the chant. CD3 26

zoo

sweet shop

café

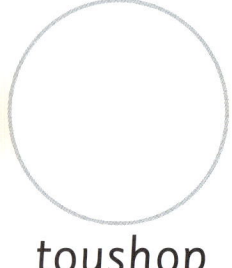
toyshop

bookshop

 Spelling: go to page 79 in your Activity Book.

Key learning outcomes: identify and say places in town; sing a song about the town
Vocabulary: places in town

1 Listen and repeat. Act out. CD3 27

ZOO

Welcome to Newtown, Tim.

Thanks, Molly.

There's a big zoo here.

Great! I love animals.

And there are two sweet shops.

Fantastic!
I love sweets, too.

Grammar

There's a zoo.
There are two sweet shops.

2 How many are there? Listen and write the number. CD3 28

 2

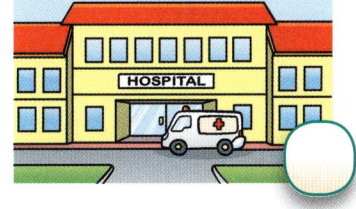

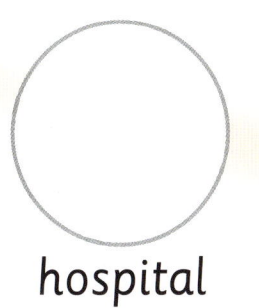

hospital

restaurant

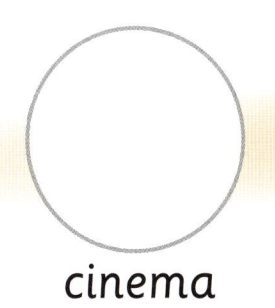

cinema

swimming
pool

supermarket

Key learning outcomes: use *There's …* and *There are …*
Grammar: *There's (a hospital). There are (two cinemas).*

7 Lesson 3 **Story**

Before you read

What places can you see in the story?

1 Listen and read. Act out. CD3 29

The treasure hunt

1

Can we explore your town today?

Yes, of course.

Look! Toby has got something in his mouth.

2

What is it?

It's a treasure map.

Well done, Toby! Let's look for the treasure.

3

First, look for a big, old tree.

There's a big, old tree next to the swimming pool.

Let's go!

4

Look! There's the old tree.

Now look for two yellow rocks.

There are two yellow rocks in front of the zoo. Come on!

Key learning outcomes: read, listen and understand a story about a treasure map
Language: *There's a tree next to / in front of … . How many steps are there?*

5
What's next, Tim?
Count 20 steps.
We can't cross the road here.

6
Magic Bike, can you help?
Wow! Now we can cross the road.

7
The man is green. Let's cross.
How many steps are there, Tim?
There are 20.
1, 2, 3, …

8
… 18, 19, 20! What can you see, Molly?
It's a big bone!
Of course! It's a dog's treasure map!

Now watch the animated story!

After you read

➡ Go to page 72 in your Activity Book.

2 **Values** Read and write.

red   yellow   green

Remember! Cross the road when the man is _____.

1 **Listen, point and say.** CD3 30

bus   boat   motorbike   train   helicopter   lorry

2 **Listen and point. Sing** *How many?*  CD3 31

Ready, Steady, Go!

How many? How many?
How many cars are there?
How many? How many?
How many cars are there?

One, two, three,
Four, five, six,
Seven, eight cars.

Nine, ten,
Eleven, twelve,
Thirteen, fourteen cars.

Fifteen, sixteen,
Seventeen, eighteen,
Nineteen, twenty cars.

There are twenty cars.
Yes, there are twenty cars.

3 **Talk Partners** **Listen and repeat. Play a memory game.** CD3 32

11  15  18

14  12  13

How many motorbikes are there?

There are 15 motorbikes.

Correct!

Key learning outcomes: ask and answer questions using *How many …?*
Vocabulary: transport; numbers 11–20 **Grammar:** *How many (cars) are there?*

1 Listen and say.  CD3 34

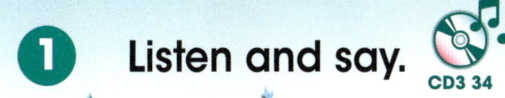

Toby's tongue twister

z – z – z. There's a lazy zebra in the zoo.

2 Listen and cross out the transport. Say *Bingo*. CD3 35

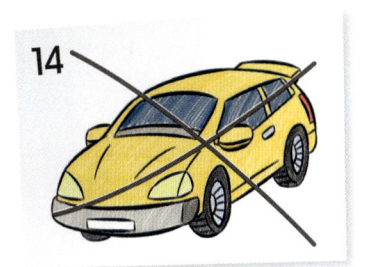

3 💬 **Talk Partners** Make the cards. Play *Bingo*.

Teacher's Resource Bank: Unit 7

There are fourteen cars.

BINGO!

Key learning outcomes: play a communication game about transport
Phonics: the 'z' sound

Lesson 6 **British culture**

1 Listen and read. Answer.  CD3 36

> Lots of people travel by bike in our town. Cycling is fun and it's good exercise, too. We love our bikes!

1 On Monday, there's a cycling class in the school playground.

2 On Saturday, we go shopping. We go to the town centre by bike with Mum.

3 This is a rickshaw. It's got three wheels. You can see our town in a rickshaw. There are lots of things to see!

4 There are lots of bikes in our town. Oh no! Where's my bike?

Think about your culture
How do you travel in your town?

Key learning outcomes: read about cycling in Britain; think about how you travel where you live

Text type: **A fable**

Before you read

1 Where do you think the mice live? Write. **town   country**

I live in the _____.

I live in the _____.

2 Listen and read the fable.  **CD3 38**

After you read

→ Go to page **76** in your Activity Book.

1 Listen and number. Write and say.  **CD3 39**

toyshop   bookshop   supermarket   hospital   zoo   café
cinema   ~~restaurant~~   sweet shop   swimming pool

_____   *restaurant*   _____   _____   _____

_____   _____   _____   _____   _____

2 What can you see in your classroom? Read, count and answer.

1 How many boards are there?

There are _____ boards.

2 How many bins are there?

There are _____ bins.

3 👥 **Cooperative learning** Sing *Well done!*  **CD3 40**

WELL DONE! GIVE ME FIVE!

Key learning outcomes: review language in the unit
Language: places in town, *How many …?* and numbers 11–20

Today's programme is about transport. How do you travel in your town?

1 Watch the video. Number the pictures. ▶

2 Watch the video again. Read and tick (✓) or cross (✗). ▶

1 The train is fast. ✓

2 The family has got one bike. ◯

3 The school bus is big and yellow. ◯

4 The brother and sister go to school by bike. ◯

3 Read and circle.

Reading digital maps

1 The supermarket is (**next to**) / **behind** the café.

2 The swimming pool is on **North Street** / **South Street**.

3 The cinema is on **Green Street** / **Blue Street**.

4 The hospital is near the **park** / **restaurant**.

You can look for places in the town with a digital map.

1 **Listen and point. Sing** *What are you wearing?*  CD3 42

What are you wearing?
Hey! Hey! Hey!
What are you wearing today?

I'm wearing shorts
And a T-shirt, too.
I'm wearing a sun hat.
What about you?

Chorus

I'm wearing a shirt
And trousers, too.
I'm wearing trainers.
What about you?

Chorus

I'm wearing a skirt
And a sweater, too.
I'm wearing shoes.
What about you?

2 **Read and stick the ten stickers. Listen and say the chant.**  CD3 44

sweater

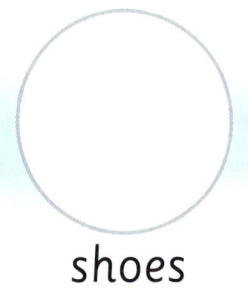
shoes

T-shirt

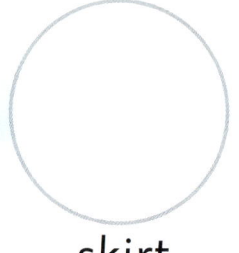
skirt

sun hat

📖 **Learning to learn** ➔ Spelling: go to page 89 in your Activity Book.

Key learning outcomes: identify and say ten items of clothing; sing a song about clothes
Vocabulary: clothes

1 **Listen and repeat. Act out.** CD3 45

Is it cold, Jake?

No, it isn't. It's hot today.

What are you wearing?

I'm wearing shorts and a T-shirt. Hurry up, Molly.

I'm coming.

Grammar

What are you wearing?
I am wearing a T-shirt.
I'm wearing a T-shirt.

2 **Listen and match.** CD3 46

1    2   3   4

a    b    c    d

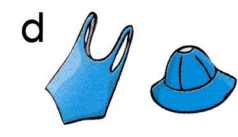

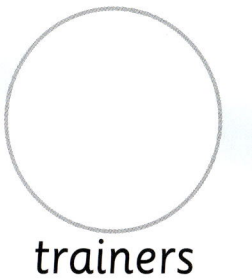 **trainers**

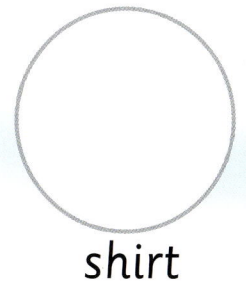 **shirt**

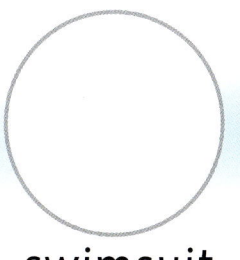 **swimsuit**

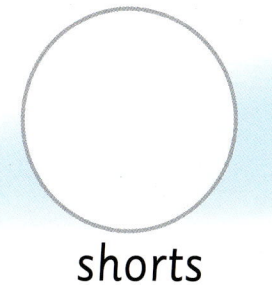 **shorts**

 **trousers**

Key learning outcomes: use present continuous to describe what you are wearing
Grammar: *What are you wearing? I'm wearing (shorts) and (a T-shirt).*

Before you read

What's the weather like in the story?

1 Listen and read. Act out. CD3 47

Fun at the camp

1

Wow! There are lots of fun activities here.

Look! She's riding a horse.

And he's sailing a boat. I love boats.

2

It's hot! Let's swim in the lake.

Good idea. Now, where's my swimsuit?

3

I'm sorry, children. You can't swim today. It's dangerous.

Bad luck.

4 The next day …

It's cold.

I'm not cold. I'm wearing trousers and a shirt. Come on! Let's ride a horse.

But it's raining, too.

Key learning outcomes: read, listen and understand a story about an activity camp
Language: *I'm wearing trousers. She's riding a horse. He's sailing a boat.*

5

I'm sorry, children. You can't ride today. It's raining.

Oh no! What a pity.

6 The next day …

Hurray! It's hot and sunny today.

Perfect! Let's sail a boat.

7

You can go in the water today, children.

Yes, but we can't sail a boat. It isn't windy.

Magic Bike, can you help?

Ring Ring Ring

8

Wheeee! This is fantastic!

Yes! We can't sail a boat …

… but we can sail the magic bike!

Now watch the animated story!

After you read

→ **Go to page 82 in your Activity Book.**

2 **Values** Read and write.

red   yellow   green

Don't go in the water when the flag is _____. It's dangerous.

Values: safety near water

1 Listen, point and say.
CD3 48

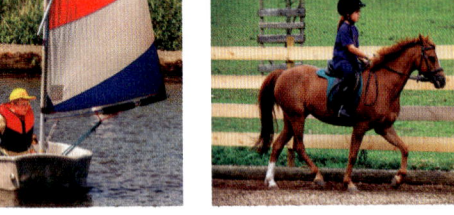

sail a boat   ride a horse   play the guitar   play volleyball   sing songs

2 Listen and point. Sing *Camping is great!*
CD3 49

*We're in a forest
Near a lake.
Camping is great.
Yes! Camping is great!*

What's Molly doing in the sun?
She's riding a horse.
She's having fun!

What's Beth doing in the sun?
She's sailing a boat.
She's having fun!

What's Jake doing in the sun?
He's playing the guitar.
He's having fun!

3 **Talk Partners** Listen and repeat. Ask and answer.
CD3 50

What's Dan doing?

He's swimming.

Key learning outcomes: ask and answer questions about what people are doing
Vocabulary: outdoor activities **Grammar:** *He's / She's (playing the guitar).*

1 Listen and say. CD3 52

Toby's tongue twister

v – v – v. **V**icky the **v**et lo**v**es **v**olleyball.

2 Listen and match. CD3 53

1 Emma

2 Ben

3 Tom

4 Susan

5 Alex

6 Mary

Teacher's Resource Bank: Unit 8

3 Talk Partners Make and play the game.

What's Emma doing?

She's swimming.

Key learning outcomes: play a communication game about what people are doing
Phonics: the 'v' sound

1 **Listen and read. Answer.** CD4 1

In the summer, we camp in the garden. It's good fun.

Dad plays the guitar, and we sing songs. My favourite song is 'Alice the camel'. It's funny.

We sleep in our sleeping bags in big tents.

At night, we tell stories. They're scary!

2 **Listen and sing** *Alice the camel*. CD4 2

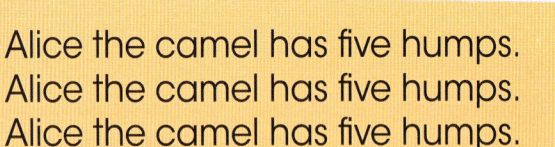

Alice the camel has five humps.
Alice the camel has five humps.
Alice the camel has five humps.

So go, Alice, go!
BOOM! BOOM! BOOM!

Alice the camel has four humps …
Alice the camel has three humps …
Alice the camel has two humps …
Alice the camel has one hump …
Alice the camel has no humps …
Now Alice is a horse!

Think about your culture
Do you go camping? What activities do you do?

Key learning outcomes: read about camping in Britain; think about what activities you do

 Text type: **A postcard**

Before you read

1 What can you see on the postcard? Circle and say.

a town   a lake

a playground   (boats)

a forest   horses

a farm

2 Listen and read the postcard. CD4 4

Dear Sally,

I'm at a fantastic campsite with my family. There's a beautiful forest and there's a big lake. There are lots of fun activities here. I swim in the lake and I sail a boat every day.

It's hot and sunny today. I'm wearing my new swimsuit.
It's purple and pink.

See you soon,

Sue

20

Sally Smith

12 Park Street

London

NE 14 16TN

After you read

→ Go to page **86** in your Activity Book.

Key learning outcomes: read and understand a postcard

1 Listen and number. Write and say.  CD4 5

trousers   shirt   sun hat   ~~T-shirt~~   shoes
swimsuit   trainers   shorts   sweater   skirt

_____   _____   _____   _____   _____

_____   _____   T-shirt   _____   _____

2 Look, read and complete.

What's Beth doing?

She's playing the _____.

What's she wearing?

She's wearing a _____.

3 👥 **Cooperative learning** Sing *Well done!* 🎵 CD4 6

WELL DONE!
GIVE ME FIVE!

Key learning outcomes: review language in the unit
Language: clothes, *What's he / she wearing?* and *He's / She's wearing …*

Today's programme is about camp activities. Do you go camping in the summer?

1 Watch the video. Tick (✓) or cross (✗). Are these activities in the video?

2 Watch the video again. Read and circle.

1 A **boy** / (**girl**) is sailing a boat.

2 The boy is wearing a **helmet** / **sun hat**.

3 The boys are **walking** / **running** in the forest.

4 The **dad** / **mum** is playing the guitar.

3 Read, think and circle.

Making choices

It's important to think before you choose.

1 It's windy. Let's play with a (**kite**) / **teddy**.

2 It's cold. Let's wear a **T-shirt** / **sweater**.

3 It's raining. Let's go to the **forest** / **cinema**.

4 It's hot. Let's wear a **sun hat** / **sweater**.

Key learning outcomes: watch and understand a video about camp activities

21st Ways of thinking: thinking before you choose

Unit 9 Day and night

1 Listen and do the actions. Sing *It's a beautiful day*.
CD4 8

I get up.
I get dressed.
I open the window and I say
It's a beautiful day.
It's a beautiful day today.

I wash my face.
I brush my teeth.
I open the window and I say
It's a beautiful day.
It's a beautiful day today.

I comb my hair.
I make my bed.
I open the window and I say
It's a beautiful day.
It's a beautiful day today.

2 Read and stick the ten stickers. Listen and say the chant.
CD4 10

get up

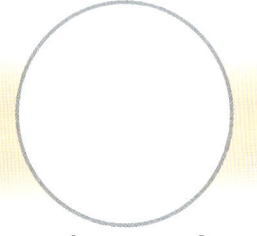
wash my face

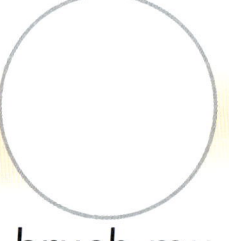
brush my teeth

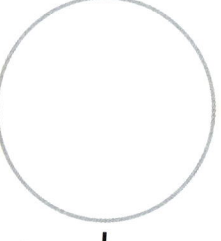
comb my hair

have a shower

 Learning to learn ➜ Spelling: go to page 99 in your Activity Book.

Key learning outcomes: identify and say ten daily routines; sing a song about daily routines
Vocabulary: daily routines

1 **Listen and repeat. Act out.**
CD4 11

I wash my face every day.

Me, too.

And I brush my teeth every day.

Me, too.

Are you ready?

Yes, I am. Let's play!

Grammar

I wash my face every day.
Me, too.

2 **Listen and tick (✓).**
CD4 12

 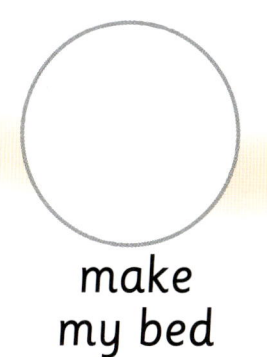   

get dressed

make my bed

go to school

go to bed

sleep

Key learning outcomes: use present simple for daily routines
Grammar: *I (wash my face) every day.*

Before you read

Where is the magic bike in the story?

1 **Listen and read. Act out.** CD4 13

The wobbly tooth

Key learning outcomes: read, listen and understand a story about a lost tooth
Language: *I have breakfast every morning.*

5

Can you see my tooth?

No, I can't. It isn't in the grass.

And it isn't in the flowers. Sorry, Jake.

6

It's time for dinner. Come in and wash your hands, please.

Great! I'm hungry.

Don't worry, Jake. We can look for your tooth tomorrow.

7

After dinner …

Look at the magic bike! What's it doing?

It's looking for your tooth, Jake.

8

Look, Jake! There's magic under your pillow.

Wow! It's my tooth. Magic Bike, you're incredible!

Now watch the animated story!

After you read

➔ Go to page 92 in your Activity Book.

2 **Values** Read and write.

teeth   feet   hands

Remember! Brush your _____ before you go to bed.

1 Listen, point and say.

breakfast in the morning

lunch in the afternoon

dinner in the evening

a snack at night

2 Listen and point. Sing *Are you hungry?*

Are you hungry in the morning?
Yes, I am. Yes, I am.
I have breakfast in the morning.
Yum, yum, yum.

Are you hungry in the afternoon?
Yes, I am. Yes, I am.
I have lunch in the afternoon.
Yum, yum, yum.

Are you hungry in the evening?
Yes, I am. Yes, I am.
I have dinner in the evening.
Yum, yum, yum.

3 **Talk Partners** Listen and repeat. Play a game.

I have lunch in the morning.

No!

I have lunch in the afternoon.

Yes!

Key learning outcomes: say when you have meals
Vocabulary: meal times   **Grammar:** *I have (dinner in the evening).*

1 **Listen and say.** CD4 18

Toby's tongue twister

th – th – th. Three **th**in tigers have a ba**th** on **Th**ursday.

2 **Listen and match.** CD4 19

1

2

3

at night

in the evening

in the morning

3 **Talk Partners** **Make and play the game.**

I get up at night.

That isn't right. My turn.

I get up in the morning.

Yes, that's right.

Key learning outcomes: play a communication game about daily routines
Phonics: the 'th' sound

1 **Listen and read. Answer.** CD4 20

In Britain, the Tooth Fairy visits children's bedrooms at night.

1

When my tooth falls out, I put it in a box. I put the box under my pillow.

2

The Tooth Fairy comes at night. She takes my tooth when I'm sleeping.

3

In the morning, I find a letter from the Tooth Fairy. The letter says 'Thank you, Lucy'.

4

I find money from the Tooth Fairy, too. I put it in my money box.

💡 **Think about your culture**
Have you got a Tooth Fairy in your country?

Key learning outcomes: read about the Tooth Fairy in Britain; think about what happens to teeth where you live

 Text type: **A poem**

Before you read

1 Listen and number. Say *day* or *night*.
CD4 21

sleep

1
owl

cockerel

children

2 Listen and read the poem.
CD4 22

Morning time

It's morning time.
The sun is in the sky.
The moon and the stars
Say goodbye.

The owl goes to sleep
With a whoo whoo.
And the cockerel crows
Cock-a-doodle-doo.

Get up, children
It's a new day.
Get up, children
It's time to play.

3 Act out the poem.

After you read

→ Go to page **96** in your Activity Book.

Key learning outcomes: read and understand a poem

1 Listen and number. Write and say.  CD4 24

> have a shower   comb my hair   ~~sleep~~   make my bed   get up
> wash my face   go to bed   get dressed   go to school   brush my teeth

_____   _____   _____   _____   _____

1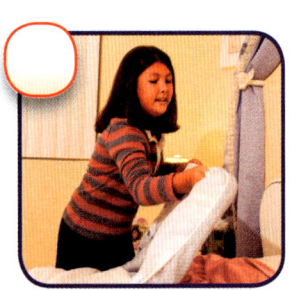

sleep   _____   _____   _____   _____

2 Look and write.

> evening   night   ~~morning~~   afternoon

1    2    3    4

1 ___morning___   2 _____

3 _____   4 _____

3 👥 **Cooperative learning** Sing *Well done!* CD4 25

WELL DONE! GIVE ME FIVE!

Key learning outcomes: review language in the unit
Language: daily routines and times of the day

Today's programme is about teeth. When do you brush your teeth?

1 Watch the video. Number the pictures. ▶

2 Watch the video again. Read and tick (✓) or cross (✗). ▶

1 The girl is eating chocolate. ✓
2 The boy is drinking juice. ◯

3 The girl is happy at the dentist. ◯
4 A boy has got a wobbly tooth. ◯

3 Read and think. Tick (✓) or cross (✗).

Looking after your teeth

It's important to look after your teeth.

1 It's important to eat healthy food. ✓

2 It's important to drink juice. ◯

3 It's important to brush your teeth. ◯

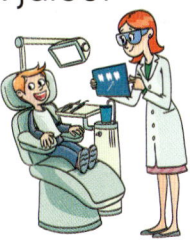

4 It's important to go to the dentist. ◯

Key learning outcomes: watch and understand a video about teeth
21st Living in the world: looking after your teeth

one hundred and one **101**

HOLIDAYS
Make a holiday list

Learn

 **1** Listen, point and say. Where do you go on holiday? Tick (✓). CD4 27

beach

mountains

city

 **2** 💬 **Talk Partners** Listen. Ask and answer. CD4 28

Where do you go on holiday?

I go to the beach. What about you?

 **3** Listen, point and say. Circle the things you use on holiday. CD4 29

boots

swimsuit

sunglasses

sweets

torch

Plan your project

 Prepare to make a holiday list. Go to page 100 in your Activity Book.

Key learning outcomes: identify and talk about holiday places and objects
Language: *Where do you go on holiday? I go to the (beach).*

Create

1 Read. Make a holiday list.

Digital tip!
You can use the Internet to find new words in English.

Use a computer to make a holiday list. Print the list out.

Decorate your list. Draw and colour pictures.

Show and tell

2 👥 **Cooperative learning** Sing *Listen to others*.  CD4 30

3 Create a class display. Listen. Tell the class about your holiday list. CD4 31

Our summer holiday lists

My holiday list
sunglasses
swimsuit
water
camera
towel
football
book
spade

My holiday list
water
sun hat
book
towel
sunglasses
sweets
bag
swimsuit

My holiday list
sun hat
water
boots
map
torch
sweater
tent
sleeping bag

I go to the beach on holiday. It's hot and sunny there. I've got a swimsuit on my list.

Have a nice holiday!

Think about your project

 Go to page 101 in your Activity Book.

Key learning outcomes: use a computer to make a holiday list and create a class display
Language: *I go to the (beach). It's (hot) there. I've got a (swimsuit) on my list.*

Bonfire Night

1 **Read and listen.** CD4 32

1

It's Bonfire Night.
I can see a big
bonfire. It's fantastic!

2

I eat a toffee apple
on Bonfire Night.
It's delicious!

3

I can see fireworks in the
sky. They're red, orange,
yellow and purple.

2 **Listen and read the action rhyme. Say and do the rhyme.** CD4 33

One big firework on the ground,
It's red and yellow, blue and brown.
1-2-3-4-5
Whoosh! It goes up to the sky.
See the stars all around.
Down they go, to the ground.

3 **Read the action rhyme again. Colour the firework.**

4 **Make a firework. Do the action rhyme with your firework.**

Teacher's Resource Bank: Festivals

 **Think about your culture**
Do you see fireworks in your country?

Key learning outcomes: say and do a firework action rhyme
Language: *I can see (fireworks). They're (red and yellow).*

Valentine's Day

1 **Read and listen.** CD4 34

> On Valentine's Day people think about the people they love.

1 I love my mother. Her name is Amanda. She helps me every day.

2 I love my grandfather. His name is Tony. We read books together.

3 I love my friend. Her name is Anna. We play in the playground at school.

2 **Who do you love? Write and draw.**

1 I love my _____.

_____ name is _____.

2 I _____.

_____ name is _____.

3 **Make a Valentine's Day card.**

Teacher's Resource Bank: Festivals

 **Think about your culture**
Do you have Valentine's Day in your country?

Key learning outcomes: think and write about the people you love
Language: *I love (my mother). She (helps me).*

1 **Listen and colour. There is one example.** CD4 35

2 **Talk Partners** **Listen and point. Ask and answer.** CD4 36

Where's the ruler?

Here.

What colour is it?

It's orange.

▶ **Watch the external exams video**

Key learning outcomes: practise for the Pre A1 Starters Listening Part 4 and Speaking Part 3

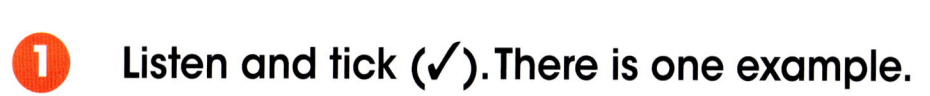
Cambridge Exams Practice: Pre A1 Starters 2

1 **Listen and tick (✓). There is one example.** CD4 37

 Listening

1 Where is the teddy?

A 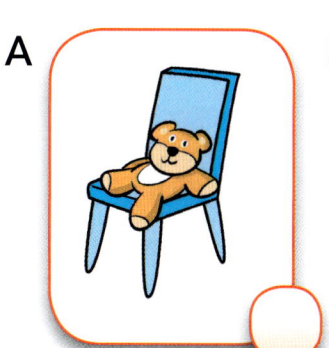 B ✓

2 What colour is the train?

A  B

3 Where is the robot?

A 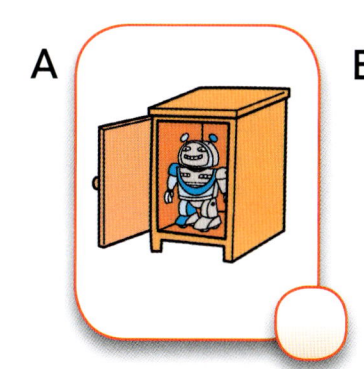 B

4 What colour is the kite?

A  B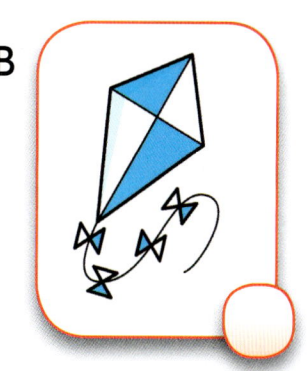

2  💬 **Talk Partners** **Listen and repeat. Ask and answer.** CD4 38

 Speaking

What's your name?

My name is Alice.

How old are you?

I'm six.

▶ Watch the external exams video

Listening

1 Listen and draw lines. There is one example. CD4 39

Lucy | Anna | Pat | Hugo

Eva | Dan | Alice

2 🗨 **Talk Partners** Listen and repeat. Ask and answer. CD4 40

Speaking

What colour is your hair?

My hair is black.

What colour are your eyes?

My eyes are brown.

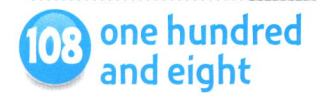 Watch the external exams video

Key learning outcomes: practise for the Pre A1 Starters Listening Part 1 and Speaking Part 4

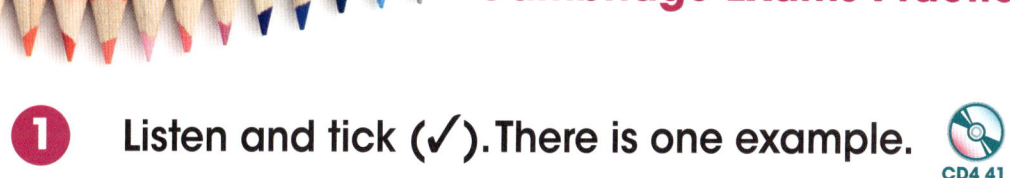

1 **Listen and tick (✓). There is one example.**  CD4 41

Listening

1 What is Bill's favourite food?

A  B  ✓

2 What is Lucy's favourite food?

A  B

3 What is Sue's favourite fruit?

A 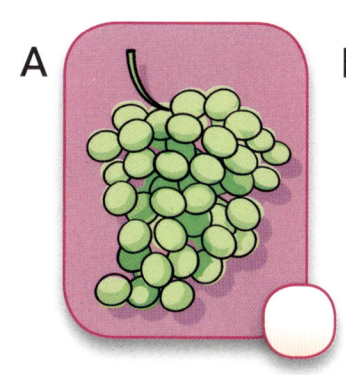 B

4 What is Sam's favourite drink?

A  B

2 🗨 **Talk Partners** **Listen and repeat. Ask and answer.**  CD4 42

Speaking

What's your favourite food?

It's ice cream. What about you? What's your favourite food?

My favourite food is chicken.

 ▶ Watch the external exams video

1 Listen and colour. There is one example.

CD4 43

Listening

2   **Talk Partners** Listen and point. Ask and answer.

CD4 44

Speaking

What's this?

It's a cow.

Tell me about it.

It's big. It's black and white. It's got four legs.

▶ **Watch the external exams video**

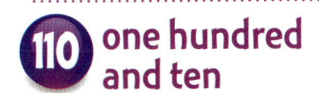

Key learning outcomes: practise for the Pre A1 Starters Listening Part 4 and Speaking Part 3

Listening

1 **Listen and tick (✓).There is one example.** CD4 45

1 Where are the cats?

A  B

2 Where is the duck?

A  B

3 Where are the birds?

A  B

4 Where is the dog?

A  B

2 **💬 Talk Partners Listen and point. Ask and answer.**  CD4 46

Speaking

Where's the blue bird? It's on the bike.

Where are the red birds? They're between the flowers.

▶ Watch the external exams video

1 Listen and colour. There is one example. CD4 47

2 💬 **Talk Partners** Listen and point. Ask and answer. CD4 48

What's this?

It's a boat.

Do you go to school by boat?

No, I don't.

▶ **Watch the external exams video**

Key learning outcomes: practise for the Pre A1 Starters Listening Part 4 and Speaking Part 3

Listening

1 **Listen and tick (✓). There is one example.**
CD4 49

1 What is Bill wearing today?

A  B  ✓

2 What is May wearing today?

A  B

3 What is Mark doing today?

A  B

4 What is Jill doing today?

A  B

2 💬 **Talk Partners** **Listen and point. Ask and answer.**
CD4 50

Speaking

What's he doing? — He's playing football.

What's he wearing? — He's wearing a T-shirt.

▶ Watch the external exams video

9

1 Listen and draw lines. There is one example.

CD4 51

Listening

| May | Mark | Alex | Sue |

| Lucy | Anna | Hugo |

2  **Talk Partners** Listen and point. Ask and answer.

CD4 52

Speaking

What's this?

Juice.

Do you have juice for breakfast?

Yes, I do.

▶ **Watch the external exams video**

Key learning outcomes: practise for the Pre A1 Starters Listening Part 1 and Speaking Part 3

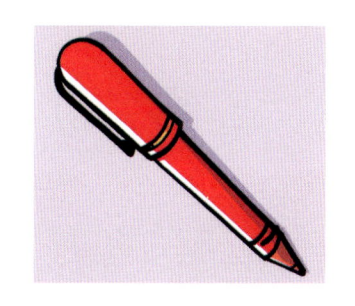

External Exams Syllabus

Unit	Cambridge Exams Practice (Pupil's Book)	Cambridge Exams Practice (Activity Book)	Trinity Exams Practice (Teacher's Resource Bank)
1	**Pre A1 Starters Listening Part 4** Task: Identifying and colouring **Pre A1 Starters Speaking Part 3** Task: Answering questions about small pictures	**Pre A1 Starters Reading and Writing Part 2** Task: Writing yes/no answers **Pre A1 Starters Reading and Writing Part 3** Task: Spelling words	**Grades 1 and 2** Stating simple facts and describing objects
2	**Pre A1 Starters Listening Part 3** Task: Multiple choice picture cloze **Pre A1 Starters Speaking Part 4** Task: Answering questions to give personal information	**Pre A1 Starters Reading and Writing Part 1** Task: Putting tick / cross answers **Pre A1 Starters Reading and Writing Part 4** Task: Cloze activity	**Grades 1 and 2** Asking simple questions and giving personal information
3	**Pre A1 Starters Listening Part 1** Task: Matching names and children **Pre A1 Starters Speaking Part 4** Task: Answering questions to give personal information	**Pre A1 Starters Reading and Writing Part 4** Task: Cloze activity **Pre A1 Starters Reading and Writing Part 1** Task: Putting tick / cross answers	**Grades 1 and 2** Asking simple questions and giving personal information
4	**Pre A1 Starters Listening Part 3** Task: Multiple choice picture cloze **Pre A1 Starters Speaking Part 4** Task: Answering questions to give personal information	**Pre A1 Starters Reading and Writing Part 2** Task: Writing yes / no answers **Pre A1 Starters Reading and Writing Part 3** Task: Spelling words	**Grades 1 and 2** Asking simple questions and giving personal information
5	**Pre A1 Starters Listening Part 4** Task: Identifying and colouring **Pre A1 Starters Speaking Part 3** Task: Answering questions about small pictures	**Pre A1 Starters Reading and Writing Part 1** Task: Putting tick / cross answers **Pre A1 Starters Reading and Writing Part 2** Task: Writing yes / no answers	**Grades 1 and 2** Stating simple facts and answering simple questions
6	**Pre A1 Starters Listening Part 3** Task: Multiple choice picture cloze **Pre A1 Starters Speaking Part 2** Task: Answering questions and talking about a big picture	**Pre A1 Starters Reading and Writing Part 5** Task: Writing one word answers **Pre A1 Starters Reading and Writing Part 1** Task: Putting tick / cross answers	**Grades 1 and 2** Indicating the position of objects and stating simple facts
7	**Pre A1 Starters Listening Part 4** Task: Identifying and colouring **Pre A1 Starters Speaking Part 3** Task: Answering questions about small pictures	**Pre A1 Starters Reading and Writing Part 3** Task: Spelling words **Pre A1 Starters Reading and Writing Part 4** Task: Cloze activity	**Grades 1 and 2** Stating simple facts and asking simple questions
8	**Pre A1 Starters Listening Part 3** Task: Multiple choice picture cloze **Pre A1 Starters Speaking Part 2** Task: Answering questions and talking about a big picture	**Pre A1 Starters Reading and Writing Part 5** Task: Writing one word answers **Pre A1 Starters Reading and Writing Part 3** Task: Spelling words	**Grades 1 and 2** Asking simple questions and stating simple facts
9	**Pre A1 Starters Listening Part 1** Task: Matching names and children **Pre A1 Starters Speaking Part 3** Task: Answering questions about small pictures	**Pre A1 Starters Reading and Writing Part 4** Task: Cloze activity **Pre A1 Starters Reading and Writing Part 2** Task: Writing yes / no answers	**Grades 1 and 2** Stating simple facts and asking simple questions

Macmillan Education
4 Crinan Street
London N1 9XW

A division of Macmillan Publishers Limited
Companies and representatives throughout the world

Pupil's Book 978-1-380-01356-9
Pupil's Book Pack ISBN 978-1-380-01349-1

Text © Donna Shaw and Joanne Ramsden 2018
Design and illustration © Macmillan Publishers Limited 2018

The authors have asserted their right to be identified as the authors of this work in accordance with the Copyright, Designs and Patents Act 1988.

This edition published 2018

First edition entitled *High Five! English* published 2014 by Macmillan Publishers Limited

All rights reserved. No part of this publication may be reproduced, stored in a retrieval system, or transmitted in any form or by any means, electronic, mechanical, photocopying, recording, or otherwise, without the prior written permission of the publishers.

Series concept design by Tom Cole
Page make-up by Anthony Godber and emc design ltd
Illustrated by Adrian Barclay, Kathy Baxendale, Sam Church, Clive Goodyer, Andy Keylock, Julia Patton, Dusan Pavlic, Ángeles Peinador, Jorge Santillán, Tony De Saulles, Eric Smith, Laszlo Veres, Sholto Walker, Matt Ward
Cover design by Bigtop Design Limited
Cover photographs by **Getty Images**/iStockphoto/Thinkstock Images/katsto80; Tom Dick and Debbie Productions
Cover illustration by Ángeles Peinador
Course consultants: Rocío Gutiérrez Burgos and Mónica Pérez Is
Picture research by Sally Cole and Fernanda Rocha / Ikonia LLC
Songs produced and arranged by Footsteps and Tom Dick and Debbie Productions

Authors' acknowledgements
The authors would like to thank everyone at Macmillan who has given help and advice throughout this project. Special thanks from Jo to Carlos, Daniel and Alex for their patience and support during this process. Special thanks from Donna to José, Elisa, Teresa and Marina for their encouragement and enthusiasm.

Acknowledgements
The publishers would like to thank the following teachers for their contribution to the project: Amanda Morrison Prince, Colegio El Parque, La Navata, Madrid; Amaya Carrera García, Colegio Santa Teresa de Jesús, Valladolid; Ana Fernández Sáez, CEIP La Encina, Las Rozas, Madrid; Aránzazu Sánchez Rodríguez, CEIP Rosa Luxemburgo, Madrid; Beatriz García Vaquero, CEIP Mariano José de Larra, Madrid; Carme Tena, Collegi Sagrada Familia, Tortosa, Tarragona; Cristina Nieto Ruíz de Gaona, CEIP Margarita Salas, Arroyo de la Encomienda, Valladolid; Estíbaliz Medina Martín, CEIP Virgen de Navalazarza, San Agustín de Guadalix, Madrid; Iratxe Zabaleta Zendagorta, Ikastola San Fidel, Guernica, Vizcaya; Lucía Soria García, CEIP Alberto Alcocer, Madrid; M.ª Carmen Lago Muñoz, CEIP Federico García Lorca, Colmenar Viejo, Madrid; Marta Moreno Arroyo, CEIP Vicente Aleixandre, Móstoles, Madrid; Susana Espinel Beneitez, Colegio Grazalema, El Puerto de Santa María, Cádiz; Susana García Pizarro, Ateneu Instructiu, Sant Joan Despi, Barcelona; Virginia Escalona Monreal, CEIP La Encina, Las Rozas, Madrid; Mónica Pérez Is, CEIP Reina Victoria, Madrid; Rocío Gutiérrez, CEIP Lepanto, Madrid; Laura Zarzuelo, Colegio Virgen de la Almudena, Collado Villalba, Madrid; Eugenio Domínguez, Colegio Virgen de la Almudena, Collado Villalba, Madrid; Silvia Díez de Rivera, Colegio Orvalle, Las Rozas, Madrid; Maite Crespo, Colegio Jesús Nazareno, Madrid; Silvia Valderrama, CEIP Benito Pérez Galdós, Arganda del Rey, Madrid; Cristina Baeza, CEIP Rosa Chacel, Collado Villalba, Madrid; Leyre Alcalde, CEIP Cortes de Cádiz, Madrid; María Andrés, Colegio Matter Inmaculata, Madrid.

The publishers would like to thank the following for permission to reproduce their images:

Alamy Stock Photo /amphotos p47(chicken and potatoes), Alamy Stock Photo/Mile Atanasov p26(scooter), Alamy Stock Photo/Rafael Ben-Ari p37(ml), Alamy Stock Photo/Juniors Bildarchiv GmbH p86(tml), Alamy Stock Photo/Nikola Bilic p47(chicken and pasta), Alamy Stock Photo/Blend Images p36(hand), Alamy Stock Photo/Petr Bonek p26(train), Alamy Stock Photo/Digifoto Bronze p16(sharpener), Alamy Stock Photo/Magdalena Bujak p104(2), Alamy Stock Photo/Catchlight Visual Services p32(blonde hair), Alamy Stock Photo/Nigel Cattlin p57(cow), Alamy Stock Photo/Richard Coombs p63(br background), Alamy Stock Photo/Vira Dobosh pp68(sticker), (swing), Alamy Stock Photo/Mark Dyball p76(boat), Alamy Stock Photo/Greg Balfour Evans p80(tcl), Alamy Stock Photo/Eye-Stock p102(boots), Alamy Stock Photo/Food and Drink Photos p57(chicken), Alamy Stock Photo/format4 p76(bus), Alamy Stock Photo/Ian Fraser pp78-79(top), Alamy Stock Photo/ImageDJ p35(mr), Alamy Stock Photo/Yulia Gapeenko p90(mcl), Alamy Stock Photo/Vladislav Gudovskiy p47(Monday salad), Alamy Stock Photo/Esa Hiltula p68(roundabout), Alamy Stock Photo/imageBROKER p54(climb), Alamy Stock Photo/incamerastock pp68(slide, play area), Alamy Stock Photo/Bjanka Kadic p80(tl), Alamy Stock Photo/Christina Kennedy p100(tc), Alamy Stock Photo/Yongyut Khasawaong p12(cupboard), Alamy Stock Photo/Ruslan Kudrin p90(ml), Alamy Stock Photo/Andrey Kuzmin p16(ruler), Alamy Stock Photo/hirun laowisit p90(tc), Alamy Stock Photo/David Lee p47(meat and rice), Alamy Stock Photo/MBI p43(br), Alamy Stock Photo/Metta foto p102(sunglasses), Alamy Stock Photo/john norman p76(train), Alamy Stock Photo/Peter Oshkai p68(rock), Alamy Stock Photo/Chris Pearsall p75(br background), Alamy Stock Photo/Myrleen Pearson p100(mr), Alamy Stock Photo/PetStockBoys p58(chicken), Alamy Stock Photo/photonic 9 p12(chair), Alamy Stock Photo/Galina Samoylovich p100(mcr), Alamy Stock Photo/Doug Schneider p63(br boy), Alamy Stock Photo/Alex Segre p80(mc), Alamy Stock Photo/Leonid Serebrennikov p68(flower), Alamy Stock Photo/Anton Starikov p90(tr), Alamy Stock Photo/Steppenwolf p80(mr), Alamy Stock Photo/T.M.O.Pictures p86(tl), Alamy Stock Photo/Stocksolutions pp40 (sticker), p48(tc), Alamy Stock Photo/SugarStock Ltd p47(carrots), Alamy Stock Photo/Aleksandr Ugorenkov p26(dinosaur), Alamy Stock Photo/vetasster p90(mc), Alamy Stock Photo/David White p85(br), Alamy Stock Photo/Zoonar GmbH p36(legs); **BananaStock** pp36(mouth, nose, eyes), 102(strawberry), 100(ml); **Comstock Images** p44(cherry), 48(tcr); **Corbis** p68(grass); **Fancy** pp56-57(top); **FLPA** /Neil Bowman p58(blackbird), FLPA/David Hosking p58(frog), FLPA/Gerard Lac p54(jump), Fotolibra/Nick Jenkins p80(ml); **Getty Images** pp16(backpack), 18, 26(ball), 44(mango, peach, lemon), 48(mr, mcr), 102(jelly beans), Getty Images/Atw Photography p47(jelly), Getty Images/BananaStock RF/Thinkstock Images p36(arms), Getty Images/Blend Images/KidStock p32(short hair), 86(tr), Getty Images/Blend Images/Jose Luis Pelaez Inc p86(tm), Getty Images/Steve Cohen p48(tr), Getty Images/Corbis/Fly Fernandez p81(mcl), Getty Images/Corbis/Fuse p44(grapes), Getty Images/Corbis/Robert Landau p68(bush), Getty Images/Creatas Video+/bowdenimages p17(mcl, mcr, r), Getty Images/Creatas video+/davincidig p27(ml), Getty Images/Creatas Video+/monkeybusinessimages p81(mr), Getty Images/Creatas Video+/SolStock p17(ml), Getty Images/Creatas Video+/Wavebreakmedia p37(mcl), Getty Images/Dorling Kindersley/Andy Crawford p26(doll), Getty Images/Dorling Kindersley/Mike Dunning p67(soil), Getty Images/Dorling Kindersley/Will Heap p67(water), Getty Images/Dorling Kindersley/Dave King p47(Friday soup), Getty Images/Dorling Kindersley/Bob Langrish p58(horse), Getty Images/Dorling Kindersley/Susanna Price p26(car), Getty Images/E+/DaveBolton p76(lorry), Getty Images/E+/Difydave p47(cake), Getty Images/E+/DonNichols p90(tl), Getty Images/E+/narvikk p58(cow), Getty Images/E+/vpopovic pp106-115(top banner),117(top banner), Getty Images/F1online/David & Micha Sheldon p57(blackbird), Getty Images/Future/T3 Magazine/Contributor p26(game), Getty Images/Hemera/Sarah Mchattie p68(seesaw), Getty Images/Image Bank Film: Signature/Dennis Welsh p69(mr), Getty Images/Image Source p76(helicopter), Getty Images/Isabel Batty/EyeEm p68(tree), Getty Images/Guerilla p105(3), Getty Images/iStock/Getty Images Plus p16(laptop), Getty Images/iStock/Getty Images Plus/Barryj13 p53(br), Getty Image/iStock/Getty Images Plus/Jmichl p58(goat), Getty Images/iStock/Getty Images Plus/kf4851 p49(mcl), Getty Images/iStock/Getty Images Plus/luismmolina p12(board), Getty Images/iStock/nycshooter p36(toes), Getty Images/iStock/Sezeryadigar p16(rubber), Getty Images/Maximilian Stock Ltd. p48(ml), Getty Images/Moment Select/Paul McGee p100(tr), Getty Images/Moment/Fidelis Simanjuntak p49(mcr, mr), Getty Images/OJO Images/David Henderson p102(mountains), Getty Images/ONOKY/Fabrice LEROUGE pp86(tmr), 91(mcr), Getty Images/PhotoDisc pp47(Thursday salad), 48(tcl), Getty Images/Photodisc/Ozgur Donmaz p76(motorbike), Getty Images/Photographer's Choice/Peter Dazeley p49(ml), Getty Images/Photographer's Choice/Darrell Gulin p67(flowers), Getty Images/Photolibrary/Elfi Kluck p89, Getty Images/Stockbyte/Jupiterimages p35(r), Getty Images/Stockbyte/Verity Jane Smith p67(seeds), Getty Images/The Image Bank/Tom Grill p67(grass), Getty Images/The Image Bank/Romilly Lockyer p38, Getty Images/The Image Bank/Superstudio p21(br), Getty Images/The Image Bank/Paul Taylor pp88-89(top banner), Getty Images/Verve/Redhot Productions p101(tcl), Getty Images/Vetta/kajakiki p91(mcl), Getty Images/Andrew Bret Wallis p47(fruit salad); **IMAGE 100** p36(ear); **Image Source** pp48(mc), 100(mc), 102(lollipop), Image Source/Jasper White CM p80(tcr); **John Foxx Images** pp54(fly), 57(dog), 58(sheep, duck); **Macmillan Publishers Ltd.** /Paul Bricknell pp8(book), 16(book), sticker(book), 26(bear), 67(book), 100(tcr), Macmillan Publishers Ltd./Paul Bricknell/Dean Ryan p47(Wednesday soup), Macmillan Publishers Ltd./Haddon Davies p90(tcr), Macmillan Publishers Ltd./Rob Judges/Des Dubber p102(torch), Macmillan Publishers Ltd./Lisa Payne pp7, 11(bl, br), 12, 13, 14, 16(crayon, pencil), 21(bl), 22, 23, 24, 31(bl), 32, 33, 34, 38(pencil), 43(bl), 44(b), 45(b), 46, 53(bl), 54(b), 55(b), 56, 63(bl), 64, 65, 66, 70(pencil), 75(bl), 77, 78, 85(bl), 86(b), 87, 88(tr,1,3), 95(bl), 96, 97, 98, 102(pencil), **Macmilan Publishers Ltd./Dean Ryan/Rob Judges p12(shelf), Macmillan Publishers Ltd./David Tolley pp90(tcl), 102(swimsuit); PhotoDisc** pp44(coconut), 102(beach); **Photospin** pp50(sticker), 58(cat); **Plainpicture** /beyond/Lea Roth p57(horse), Plainpicture/Folio Images/Peter Cederling p35(ml), Plainpicture/Glasshouse/Eric Schwortz p102(city), Plainpicture/Helge Sauber pp66-67(top), Plainpicture/Reilika Landen p80(mcl), Plainpicture/OJO/Robert Daly pp46-47(top), Plainpicture/Stock4B p36(feet); **Shutterstock** /Adisa p68(bush), Shutterstock/Aedka Studio p27(mcl), Shutterstock/akennedy1 p59(mcl), Shutterstock/anakondasp p54(run), Shutterstock/asiastock p54(walk), Shutterstock/BlackMac p69(mcr), Shutterstock/Andrew Burgess p39(tr), Shutterstock/Coprid p90(mcr), Shutterstock/CreativeZone p69(ml), Shutterstock/diamant24 p48(mcl), Shutterstock/DPS p101(tl), Shutterstock/Elmtree p59(mr), Shutterstock/ponazhev evgeniy p37(mcr), Shutterstock/Gelpi p32(brown hair), Shutterstock/GLF Media pp59(mcl), 37(mr), Shutterstock/Horus2017 p47(meat and vegetables), Shutterstock/JPC-PROD pp24-45(top banner), Shutterstock/Karkas pp82(sticker), 90(mr), Shutterstock/LDprod p105(1), Shutterstock/Kino Masterskaya p27(mr), Shutterstock/mikeledray p48(tl), Shutterstock/Monkey Business Images pp81(ml), 91(mr), 105(2), Shutterstock/MsMaria p70(tl), Shutterstock/nikolaich p26(kite), Shutterstock/yotin Pakthongchai p104(3), Shutterstock/Ronnachai Palas p101(tcr), Shutterstock/Pavel L Photo and Video p81(mcr), Shutterstock/phloen p46(baked beans), Shuttestock/prapann p16(pen), Shutterstock/paul Prescott p101(tr), Shutterstock/Daxiao Productions p32(black hair), Shutterstock/schubbel p59(ml), Shutterstock/stockyimages p105(tr), Shutterstock/Sunychka Sol pp72, 80(tr), Shutterstock/The Factory p91(ml), Shutterstock/Max Topchii p95(br), Shutterstock/LeksusTuss p34-35(top banner), Shutterstock/Vladvm p16(pencil case), Shutterstock/Tracy Whiteside pp28(bl), 36(head), Shutterstock/Yuran-78 p27(mcr), Shutterstock/Rudmer Zwerver p58(mouse), Shutterstock/3DDock p12(bin), Shutterstock/3103 p12(desk); **Stockbyte** p26(robot); **Superstock** /agf photo p47(ice cream), Superstock/Blend Images pp32(long hair), 100(mcl), Superstock/ClassicStock.com p32(red hair), Superstock/Food and Drink pp47(fruit, fish and salad), Superstock/F1 ONLINE p80(mcr), Superstock/imageBROKER p54(swim), Superstock/Pixtal p67(sun), Superstock/Stock Connection p31(br), Superstock/Leonard Pine/Cultura Limited p104(1); **123RF** /sakkmesterke p69(mcl).

Photographs re-used on stickers: Alamy Stock Photo; BananaStock; Comstock Images; Corbis; FLPA; Fotolibra; Getty Images; Image Source; IMAGE 100; John Foxx Images; Macmillan Publishers Ltd.; Photospin; Plainpicture; Shutterstock; Stockbyte; Superstock.

Commissioned photography by Lisa Payne pp7, 11(bl, br), 12, 13, 14, 21(bl), 22, 23, 24, 31(bl), 32, 33, 34, 44, 45, 46(b), 53(bl), 54, 55(bl), 55, 56, 63, 64, 65, 66, 77, 78, 85, 86, 87, 88, 95, 96, 97, 98, 105, 106, 107, 108, 109, 110, 111, 112, 113, 114 and Tom Dick and Debbie Productions pp17(t, bl), 27(t, bl), 37(t, bl), 38(br, bl), 39, 49(t, bl), 59(t, bl), 69(t, bl), 70(mr, ml), 71, 81(t, bl), 101(t, bl), 102(mr, ml), 103.

These materials may contain links for third party websites. We have no control over, and are not responsible for, the contents of such third party websites. Please use care when accessing them.

Printed and bound in Uruguay

2022
17

Unit 1

Unit 2

Unit 3

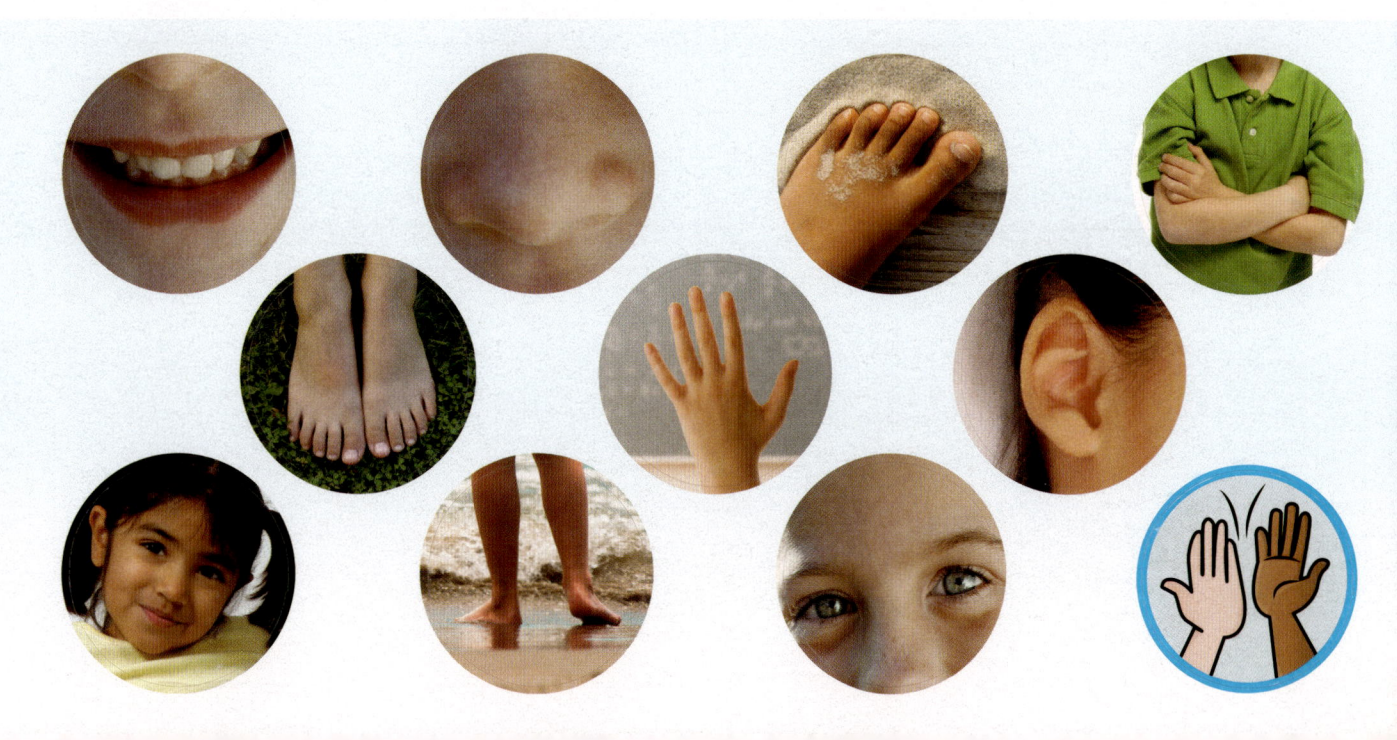

Unit 4

Unit 5

Unit 6

Unit 7

Unit 8

Unit 9